An Arcadian Awakening

Liturgy of the Fellowship of Isis
By: Olivia Robertson

FOI-Crossroads Media

© 2011-2017 Olivia Robertson & FOI-Crossroads Media.
All rights reserved.

ISBN-13: 978-1534861404
ISBN-10: 1534861408

Text and illustrations by Olivia Robertson.
Back cover photo of Olivia Robertson by FOI-Crossroads Media.

Manufactured and distributed through CreateSpace Independent Publishing Platform.

No part of this publication may be reproduced or transmitted in any form or by any means, electronic or mechanical, without written permission.

http://www.fellowshipofisis.com

ASET SHEMSU – THE RETINUE OF ASET
Aset t fem. det. shm s w "go, walk" det. plural sign

TABLE OF CONTENTS

CHAPTERS	PAGE
Preface	1
Introduction	2

Rites:

Introduction to Chapter 1. *Visions.*	5
Chapter 1. Korea	10
Intro. to Chapter 2. *Valhalla. The Golden Apples of Eternity.*	18
Chapter 2. Iceland	23
Introduction to Chapter 3. *The Magic Wood*	32
Chapter 3. Hawaii	35
Introduction to Chapter 4. *The Enchanted Doorway.*	44
Chapter 4. Utah.	47
Introduction to Chapter 5. *Where is Bohemia?*	57
Chapter 5. Bohemia.	60
Introduction to Chapter 6. *We are all Gods. So is the Cat.*	70
Chapter 6. Yucatan.	73
Introduction to Chapter 7. *Living in a Virtual World.*	82
Chapter 7. Eire.	85
Intro. to Chapter 8. *To Evolve Through Wider Consciousness.*	93
Chapter 8. Azores.	96
Intro. Chapter 9. *To Touch One Heart is to the Touch the World.*	104
Chapter 9. Glastonbury.	107

Introduction to Chapter 10. *We are Wanderers*.	117
Chapter 10. Zimbabwe.	120
Preface to Chapter 11. *The Medusa Labyrinth Trial*.	129
Introduction to Chapter 11. *It's a long way to Tipperary*.	130
Chapter 11. Crete.	132

Illustrations:

"Athena of Arcadia"	cover
"Pele, Brigid and Yemaya"	preface
"Mago as Circling Comet Belt"	4
"Pia Kong-Ju Consoles Her Daughter"	9
"Vala of the Pole Star"	17
"The One-Eyed God"	22
"The Blue Heaven"	31
"Goddess Uta-Ha"	43
"Sophia, the Lion and the Rose"	56
"Maya and Her Firebird"	69
"The Charm of Wings"	81
"The Disc Player"	92
"Cup of Tears"	103
"Leesa and Mwe"	116
"Mask of the Medusa"	128
FOI Manifesto	137

Acknowledgements:

Ritual 11, "Crete", was the last chapter written by Olivia Robertson for the book "Athena" before she passed to Spirit Sphere on November 14, 2013. Our sincere thanks to the Durdin-Robertson family to be able to publish this book, as well as all of the Fellowship of Isis Liturgy.

Special thanks as well to Minette Quick of the Circle of Brigid for sharing the majority of the artwork in this book, created by Olivia Robertson, from her personal collection.

THE STAR OF ISHTAR AND THE WEB OF THE UNIVERSE
TIAMAT DRAGON AROUND THE DIVINE MATRIX

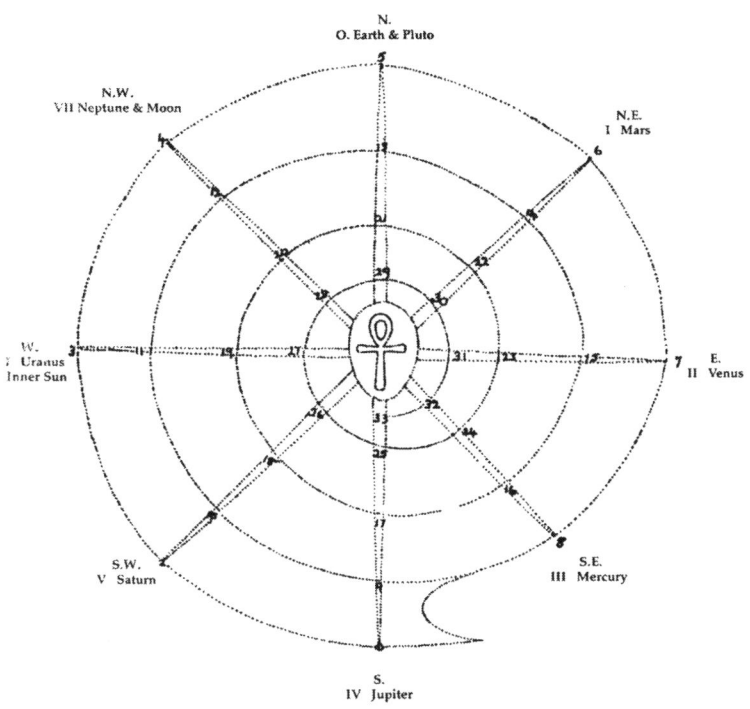

Ishtar and Tiamat are Babylonian Goddesses. The four spiral loops of the Dragon Tiamat illustrate four stages of consciousness. Physical-Etheric, Astral and Psychic, Spiritual and Divine, the latter encircling the Matrix, Source or Creation. The famous eight-pointed Star of Ishtar represents seven Cosmic Rays. 0 refers to a previous spiral, and 8 the higher octave begins a further spiral beyond. The diagram may be coloured around a white centre, moving inwards from violet, indigo, blue, green, yellow, orange, red, and again violet, the latter indicating a further inner rainbow. The diagram and key were given to Olivia Robertson through inspiration. The artwork is by Chesca Potter.

"Pele, Brigid and Yemaya"

PREFACE

Rejoice! The Goddesses and Gods are real!

The word "worship", which once meant respect, has been a barrier to communion with Deities. How can perfected Beings commune with us when we offer them obsequious prostration, with all our psychic senses closed down?

The Rainbow Flow of Divine Life, circulates through inter-communion spirals, pervading all beings. As we progress, we extend this awareness from Spirit Guides to the sphere of Angels and Devas who are advanced beyond us, and are therefore our teachers. The culmination of Divine Beings emanating from a Heavenly Sphere comes when we are ready for it, and can enjoy it. In Heaven there is no fear, nor evil. Why should we object to various names religious people give to these beings? For instance, the one I call the Wanderer, the Shamanic Deity, is known in the North as Odin; to Greeks as Zeus, and to the ancient Irish as the Dagda Mor. The name of the companion who assists the Wandering Shaman is known as Baldour the Beautiful, Mercury, Hermes, or Aengus Og.

Let us enjoy the reality of the whole company of heaven, without religious conflict.

All beings are part of the cosmic hierarchy.

Olivia Robertson
July 14, 2013

INTRODUCTION
"SACRED PLACES."

All Ancient Faiths had deep roots in some earthly home, which meant the mother to them. We think of Jerusalem, Mecca, Glastonbury, The Great Pyramid, and above all the Sphinx.

I, Olivia, was told from Spirit, in 1948, that my brother and I were to work for a Centre of Light at Clonegal. Clonegal is a mile from the meeting of the waters, where the castle is built, and where the river of healing, the Slaney, is joined by the river of the Oak, the River Derry. Where they join, there is an island of swans. In a vision, I was shown by angelic beings, a view of the castle from the sky. Light poured from the castle, and, I gathered the source of the light was from the well of Truth, St. Brigid's Holy Well.

For some years, my brother worked on energy coming from the granite from which the castle is built. Some underground source of psychic power, and also the white and silver power, like water, descending from the sky into the well. My brother was told from Spirit, that the well was for the healing of Ireland, and that the rainbow colours emanating from the dark, black earth energy from underneath the dungeon, was for the world. We were told to welcome people from all over the world, for healing, blessing, and psychic vision.

At this time of the New Aeon, 2013, I feel we are to activate this sacred place of Dana, Tara, and Brigid, Daneann goddesses of Ireland. All three have come to me in visions along with the Archangel Michael and the God Aengus Og.

On the grounds, at an angle to the Castle, is the Old Abbey ruin, with a magnificent stone altar. These act as Priory of the Noble Order of Tara. We have performed there ceremonies regularly. The grove of trees in the wilderness near the lake and the island which is the cauldron of the God Dagda, and river Derry of the Goddess Morrigan; this is the Grove of the Druid Clan of Dana, where ceremonies have been held for many years.

The rainbow Circle of Brigid have the honour of giving forth the well water to those in need. Each cup represents the Holy Grael of the New Aeon. All members spread Brigid's rainbow rays throughout the world for healing, sent forth with wisdom and love. Any solitary member can enjoy the healing and vision from the well and from the rainbow rays of Brigid: Love, Beauty and Truth.

Olivia Robertson
June 20, 2013

"Mago as Circling Comet Belt"

INTRODUCTION TO CHAPTER 1
"VISIONS."

So often I have wondered why mystical awakenings, direct revelation from Deities and Prophets, Divine Guidance, have led enthusiasts to burn, torture, blow up, brain-wash their fellows in religious fervour. I should know. I was brought to Ireland aged eight in 1925 and found religion flourished here. I had never met religious people before.

In Reigate, England, we casually attended St. Peter's Church and sang Victorian hymns without fervour. Admittedly, my Nanny informed me that if I wriggled in the pew the white-robed vicar would put me in a fiery pit. But my father, when I queried this, assured me that as Nanny thought the moon was made of green cheese, I could ignore her information. Anyway, she showed no sign of attacking non-believers. Really, there were no obvious non-believers, as we all were. We attended Christmas children's plays, vaguely thought that the Church of England was like a nice safe pair of carpet slippers, a "just in case" scenario in case there was a hell. You were expected to be nice, and good to the poor and not steal and usually speak the truth. Life was so benign and easy in Reigate – like my favourite "Just William" stories: like my beloved Tiger Tim's Weekly. Georgie Giraffe and Joey the Parrot and others were so jolly. So was Mrs. Bruin, whose only punishment was to put the eight of the boys in one bed and give them "gruel".

So I was totally taken aback to find myself in a land where religion really mattered. In Reigate I had liked Poppy Day and wore a poppy on 11th November, Armistice Day. But here some people put razors behind their poppies to cut off the fingers of enemies who tried to tear them off. The Others were Roman Catholics and Irish and some wore Easter Lilies in Easter week.

When they had got rid of the British (Us), I learnt fairly soon that our country had been cut in half. The top bit was Protestant and British with some who planted bombs. Where I lived was Roman Catholic and Irish. We Protestants did not need to plant bombs because we had most of the money, and big houses, though some of our houses were blackened shells, burnt by the Others.

I had always hoped we in the island could stop being religious. We could give up patriotism as well and turn into socialists. Instead, from the "sixties" onwards we had a thirty-year cruel, civil war. The hatred still smoulders.

In 1976 my brother, a Rector, and my sister-in-law of Quaker family, initiated the Fellowship of Isis. This we did not because of theology, or politics. We had Divine Inspiration. And awakening was happening all over the world. It was after the Second World War. The awakening was accelerated through millions of young people the world over. Later a fundamentalist return to main-stream religions was spreading with startling fanaticism. So what was happening, and what should we do about it?

I had myself gained the 3 drops of Cerridwen, Welsh Goddess of the Cauldron of Inspiration, Prophecy, and Shape-shifting. So have thousands. Empathy is our word for shape-shifting, coming through Omnipresence.

We who have in some degree experienced the Awakening, whatever we call it – Satori, Samadhi, Ecstasis, The Tao - can no longer just be happy ourselves, and run courses for enquirers. The danger of introverted living as a mystic loner is that one can develop paranoia – conspiracy terrors. It is a vagary of the psychic sense. In the Centre of the Labyrinth of Life is a monster, the Minotaur – a sinister conspirator, a black magician – what people most fear.

It was in Clonegal that I received revelation about the Labyrinth of Life. A woman from Europe came up to the Castle and asked for a course in witchcraft. She had inquired as to my whereabouts to an ancient inhabitant, who said: "I wouldn't go the Castle. Miss Olivia is a witch!" She replied: "I wish to learn to be a witch." And found her way to me.

Now I am not a professional witch, but I will take on anything. I said I'd give her a weekend course. This took place in our Church of England chapel within the Castle. We had not yet developed a Temple of Isis. At first things went swimmingly. I got her into light trance. She was extremely intelligent – naturally. She was a University lecturer. Then came challenge! Suddenly she announced: "I see the devil!"

I felt insulted. How dare she introduce the devil into our chapel! I asked Isis for guidance. I received an unexpected instruction. "Ask her, who is the devil!" I asked. She replied with venom: "He is my professor!" At once I understood the meaning of the monster in the labyrinth. Within the heart of the Labyrinth is the Mirror of the Gorgon. The monster is - yourself. The soul creates its projections, bad or good.

When you realise this, you learn to recognise the Divine in others, and honour it in yourself. Evil is only a shadow in our transient world, a reflection. We are all born of the Divine Mother, from atom to Deity.

The encouragement is that only the Divine is real. Our terrors, hatred, jealousy, ambition are nightmares that vanish when we see with the light of Truth, and feel in the darkness the heart of Love.

The first revelation of great religions came with Glory, Salvation, Heaven. I notice there is a second flow of revelation that brings a return to Nature. Physical being is honoured not despised. It is the difference between the philosopher Montaigne, who wondered what his cat was thinking – and Descartes who thought all progress came from the human mind. Hence cats had no souls. This became doctrine!

So I asked for guidance as to what to do next. My formula is simple: "Oh Isis, I am empty. Fill my emptiness." You do need to specify the Deity invoked – or you might get filled by someone you do not want . . .

I thought of all practitioners of the Arts. The Impressionists did not blow up the Academy nor writers shoot their critics, much as they may have wished to do so. Sir Christopher Wren did not burn down the old Gothic St. Paul's. So these were the people I thought sane.

Ah – where are the Companions? Where did they live? I realised that was simple. Wherever the eccentric animal-lover, Elizabeth of Bohemia dwelt, there was Bohemia. Bohemia started as her own country, and spread all over the world. "La Boheme" is the world's most loved opera – about artists. The heroes were artists pawning their coats to eat, burning their epic poems to keep warm. Yes, Bohemia is all over the western world, and similar places may be found in Tokyo, Peking, Moscow, Port Harcourt in Nigeria, Seattle, USA, and Big Island, Hawaii. They are Oases for eccentrics.

I like the tale of Quan Yin, Goddess of Compassion, who, when invoked by a sufferer, was in such a hurry to help that she even neglected to put on her make-up. Now I call that dedication.

My new book concerns Spiritual Awakening through the Arts. We learn of the work of Elaine and Aiden, now qualified Alchemists in the FOI Priesthood. I found I could not part with their doings! They run gatherings of Arcadians in many countries. It is very simple. No subscriptions, no rules, no dogma, no personal probings – just expenses covered and exchange of art gifts. "Be yourself," they declare. "You are free to find your Divinity."

"Pia Kong-Ju Consoles Her Daughter"

CHAPTER 1: KOREA
"MAGOLAND"

VISITANTS: PATH GUIDE, ELAINE, PRIESTESS OF ALCHEMY. HELPER, AIDEN, PRIEST OF ALCHEMY. DEIRDRE, ORACLE.

TEMPLE OF ARTS - KOREA

ELAINE *(PATH GUIDE)*: For those who are new to our spiritual family, we have no regulations, no vows, no secrecy. We have accepted the invitation to join this group of Arcadians to find our own truth, our own love, our own home. This we do because each of us has some divinely inspired art that we love to practise. Art used to be denigrated as only the "handmaid" to religion. We feel religion is the ground for spiritual arts, awakening in us through our own originality. We have the courage to be ourselves.

AIDEN *(HELPER)*: We are happy to have been invited to this Temple of Arts in Korea. Here we are! May the member who has welcomed us stand forth and speak!

PIA *(STANDS FORTH)*: It amuses me that you assume I can speak, let alone be original! Well, I suppose I am unique. Or so they say. I am the only authenticated autistic person in our part of the world that has recovered!

AIDEN: We would love you to describe what it was like to be autistic – and how you recovered. Are you willing to tell us, for our magazine and website?

PIA: Gladly, a bit of incense, candles and soft music would help.

MUSIC AND INCENSE. CANDLES ARE LIGHTED.

PART ONE: NARRATION

PIA: I was born entrapped as if in a glass bottle. It surrounded me on every side. This was my world. Beings could get through the glass walls with food. But they were to me just ghosts. I cared nothing for them. I could see them weep and even hear them make sounds. But otherwise I lived in a dreamy state, entirely by myself. I wanted nothing.

One of these beings took me by the hand one spring day and led me to a grass field where there was a little stream. I was quite safe – it was only a few inches deep. She left me seated on the grass, still as always. I did not feel myself to be alone. I was always alone.

Suddenly a bright bird splashed into the water out of a pool made by the rivulet. It was an orange and blue bird. Its flight made the bamboos shake to and fro with a hissing sound. And as I listened to the breeze I knelt down and gazed at my face reflected in it. As the ripples made my face quiver, I was surprised to see two large tears run down my face.

Then a wonder happened. A woman's face, divinely beautiful, appeared behind my own reflection. I looked up and jumped to my feet. A lady as beautiful as the full moon was standing - or rather hovering - just above the grasses. Her face was milky white and her scarlet lips were parted in a gentle smile. Her hair was as black as night, coiled like snakes above her head and round her shoulders. She was holding a fan in one hand and a mirror in the other.

"My dearest daughter, Pia," she said; "You have grown up in holy innocence that you may most effectively show my countenance to those who need our help. I am the Goddess Pia Kong Ju, Bodhisattva of Compassion. Look in my mirror, at yourself as Mystic Dancer."

She showed me the silver mirror, and within I saw the most beautiful country full of green trees and bright flowers, and happy children laughing and playing. Venerable grandparents sat at ease at a table piled high with fruit. And I was actually dancing!

"Oh, I want to get there!" I cried. "Please take me there!"

The Lady said: "Not so easy is it, little Pia, to reach this sacred place. It is called Magoland. This was the holy Heaven from which the people of earth were banished for bad behaviour. They were expelled by the Goddess of the land, Mago. I must leave you now. When the time comes you will be guided to reach Magoland, if you overcome various tribulations. Remember: Do good. Speak the Truth. Share with others."

Whereupon the Goddess vanished, leaving behind the holy scent of incense.

AIDEN: This time is auspicious for your trials! The full moon shines on this lovely sanctuary. Are you willing to enter trance and face the ordeals set for you?

PIA: I live for this. I long for Heaven.

ELAINE: So be it. I shall be your Path Guide. First, we need to invoke the aid of the Goddess Mago through our Priestess Deirdre in trance. She is a Priestess Alchemist, well versed in her vocation.

PART TWO: ALCHEMICAL RITE

VEILED PRIESTESS IN TRANCE.

ELAINE: Holy Goddess Mago, miracle of beauty and love, upholder of the Truth, we pray for your Oracle.

ORACLE OF THE GODDESS MAGO

Meaningless is the Heaven which you have not earned. You need to give as well as receive, travel as well as rest, and heal as well as be healed. The lost Heaven you lament is mourned with many names throughout the green earth. As innocent children you live in Heaven until you begin to grow – as do all elements, plants, animals. You find your divine self is original from Deity. So you face rivalry, passions, ideas. And this is good. Now humans have reached the final end of their solitary struggles. They were imprisoned in glass cages of separate selves. Now those outside such cages come to help those who long to escape. This is the End and the Beginning.

My Divine Manifestation appears as a mighty comet encircling the sky, with golden head and a long sweeping trail of many coloured stars. Thus I represent your Galaxy. But I also come as a child, or a poor old woman. Offer honour to all, for all are born of Divinity.

AIDEN: We give thanks to the Goddess Mago for Her Oracle.

ELAINE *(TO PIA)*: Pia, around you is the mighty galactic Goddess Mago. You have had your Vocation from the Goddess of Compassion, Pia Kong-Ju for whom you are named. Now are you willing to receive my human help as Path Guide, and enter into trance?

PIA: With all my heart.

ELAINE: You will not totally lose consciousness, because your soul will be in charge to make choices. You chose to come out of autism. Now you wish to emerge from this dream of earthly life to greater reality. So lie on the couch and close your eyes . . . You will tell us what befalls you. We shall accompany your journey as your spiritual family, but may not intervene. Otherwise the trials would have no meaning. You need to relive your life but now help others instead of doing nothing.

MUSIC.

TRANCE JOURNEY TO MAGOLAND

ELAINE: Pia, you find yourself once again at the beautiful rivulet that you love. * * *Are you there?

PIA: Yes. I am really there! How wonderful. And it is not Autumn like here. It's Spring – my favourite time. * * *

ELAINE: Tell us what happens to you. Take your time . . . We have all the time in the world. * * *

PIA: Yes. I have been here for ages and ages. * * * Oh dear. The weather is changing. It has become winter. Help! This is winter. I'm dying of cold. I'm inside some sort of glass coffin.

AIDEN: Ask Pia Kong-Ju to save you.

PIA: I call to her. But she doesn't come. Everything is changing like a film. It's too hot now, in a stuffy room. A fat woman is pressing me to her. It's horrible. I wish she'd go away. I want to go back to the field. But she won't let me go. And a nasty little boy is pinching me. He keeps chanting: "Pia is an imbecile! Pia is an imbecile!" I wish I was not here. * * * I want to tell him that I am not here, I am somewhere else. I want to escape from this stuffy room and stupid children and this fat woman who is crying and crying all over me.

So I pull a wonderful silver-white veil round me and I am safe. I can't hear or see these people – I don't care what they do or say. I can't feel the woman's tears or the boy's pinch or his silly song. If I wait long enough I'll get to the stream and I'll get in and wash myself. They've captured me in this room.

Then I remember a voice telling me to ask Pia Kong-Ju for help. So I stop being angry and ask for help. Suddenly I notice that the boy who is chanting the ugly words is hideous! No one likes to look at him. He has a hare-lip. I want to tell the woman it can be put right in a hospital. I feel sorry for him. So I throw away my white veil. I come up to him and put my arms round him and though his face looks so dreadful – I give him a hug and big kiss! I hear the woman start shouting: "A miracle! Pia Kong-Ju has heard my prayers! My little girl is cured." The boy has suddenly changed into the beautiful Goddess herself! She is laughing. "Don't judge by appearances, Pia," she says. "You have passed your first trial to reach Magoland. You have put aside your veil of seclusion."

I am overcome with joy and I look around to find a wonderful land. It has become very cold.

Where am I? I know. It is a school playground. The children are surrounding a girl who is crying. She looks different from us. We have beautiful raven-black hair and golden skin – the way the Creators made us to be. But she has a terrible skin covered with orange spots, green eyes, a huge mouth – and worst of all, bright red fuzzy hair which the children are pulling. They are saying: "She is a monster, a demon from outer space!" I know devils have red hair. But I notice she is a very brave demon, trying not to cry. I like the way she throws back her head and answers back. I still protect myself with the white veil from demons. They are so many. But now I throw it off and I put my arm round the girl. I shout out: "Look out for what you are doing! It's blasphemy to insult the Great Goddess Mago! She put us out of Heaven for insulting manners." They look scared. I explain: "Mago has red-gold hair like the sun and her body is made of white light and orange stars. What is ugly to us people is beautiful for a Goddess. If we want to go back to Heaven we had better mend our manners."

And they do. They creep away, silent. But what is very strange and wonderful, is that as the children run off, the girl turns and looks at me. She becomes as tall as a willow tree and bright as the stars. Her hair is flying around her like sun-beams. Her voice is deep and loving: "Dearest brave little Pia, thank you so much for looking after my daughter Mago. This is her first visit to earth and she is sensitive to unkindness. You have passed your second ordeal to reach my lovely land." She fades like an amber dawn into the sky * * * I feel ashamed that before I did not help her daughter. But now I really have!

I hope I can now reach Magoland – but I find myself in a very different place. I feel afraid that I might like the garish lights and too loud music and all the drunk people dancing around in a silly way. I don't want to grow up. So I draw my white veil around me so that the men will not see me and ask me to dance.

But then I see a young man who is trying to hide a tear. His hand is shaking as he wipes his face with a dirty handkerchief. He turns sideways and I see he has a crooked back. I hear one girl saying to another: "I wonder a hunchback should come to a dance. It makes it embarrassing for us having to refuse him."

Without thinking I throw aside my white veil and I approach the young man. I say: "I've never been to a dance before. I'm so clumsy, you see. I get laughed at. But would you care to show me the steps?"

His whole face lights up and he looks so joyful and loving. He puts his arm around me and says: "Pia, I was not allowed to help you. But now I can. You have passed your final test. You may enter Magoland," he says. He is Aiden, The Helper! "You have learnt to help with kindness."

But what is so extraordinary is that Magoland is the same as this dance hall. The people are kind and beautiful, the music is dreamy, the lights soft. But even as I look around wanting to make friends – I find I am back on the school playground. I see the red-haired girl join in a circle game with the others. * * * I hear the voice of the fat lady and she is talking to her son, his hare-lip cured. "Who would think my poor autistic Pia would turn into a wonderful Temple dancer. Even people in other countries have heard of her. They even visit us here . . . "

Now I understand. Where you are depends on who you are. The Goddess is everywhere – when I recognise her. When I look out of the window and see sun, moon and stars, I see Mago. Also, I see good all around me.

END OF TRANCE.

PIA SLOWLY RETURNS FROM TRANCE. REPORTS ARE SHARED. A KOREAN FEAST IS ENJOYED. THANKS ARE GIVEN TO THE DEITIES. EXCHANGE OF ARTWORKS. PIA GIVES A DANCE AND THE VISITORS A PAINTING.

End of Rite.

Sources: "Korean Folk Tales." "Small Magical Fairy Tales", with paintings, Heidi Tordrup. "The Dreaming Child," Isak Dinesen, Penguin Books, London. "The Noh Plays of Japan," Seami. trans. Waley, Grove Press, New York. "The Rainbow People", Laurence Yep, Harper Trophy, New York. "Goddesses of China, Goddesses of India, Tibet, China, Japan", Lawrence Durdin-Robertson. From Chinese poetry: "The Woman with the Caterpillar Eyebrows." "The Water Babies," Charles Kingsley. "The Star Child" from the "Complete Fairy Tales of Oscar Wilde". "Diary of a Midget," John Masefield.

"Vala of the Pole Star"

INTRODUCTION TO CHAPTER 2
"VALHALLA."
"THE GOLDEN APPLES OF ETERNITY."

When we were very young, in a country town in England – Reigate – my brother Lawrence and I would try and stop time. We could not understand where yesterday had gone to. Can you yourself? What was living reality, a place where you hurt yourself, were happy, read your comic "Tiger Tim's Weekly"– suddenly became a pale grey nothingness, "yesterday". Grown-ups did not seem to worry. We did mind. So we determined to stop time by remembering a string of happenings "now" and keep them from turning into "yesterday". Some of the list I do remember! It began: "I remember a man on a bicycle wearing a straw hat. I remember a little girl in a blue bonnet. I remember a stone called Tommy." But it was no good. Rather like reciting a creed in church, it was a string of words, but where was the man in a straw hat?

We thought of watching water flow past us in a stream, and try and follow a floating straw. No use. The straw was real in NOW – and then was lost in "yesterday". Grown-ups kept collections of photos of people in ancient uniforms, huge hats – long skirts, and blank-faced children now all lost in time.

There were accounts of heaven if you behaved and hell if you didn't. But no-one had actually been there.

As I grew up I learnt there were some people who had been there – and come back. This behaviour was regarded as an unhealthy occupation, reserved for Saints, lunatics and imposters. And it was this hard core of fear and therefore rejection that interested me as I grew up.

You see nearly everybody was dead. A long line of Kings, Queens, the great and the good or bad – and un-numbered people commemorated statistically on cenotaphs and churchyards. I imagined a milling crowd of ghosts which I was told were hallucinations or undesirable residents, mainly in old country houses, including ours. I noticed such family ghosts with their portraits were accepted as a social asset: "Sir Humphrey appears in this passage every November."

To curb any investigation by amateurs, dealings with Spirits were the correct task of priests and gurus. Such experts were usually dead for hundreds of years. Hence their information was coded and infallible.

Why not become a modern expert? It is possible now because one is not in danger of hanging or burning for heresy. But new scientific attitude had a more insidious weapon to prevent illicit ventures into other dimensions. Ridicule. Disbelief. This could destroy one's reputation. Even then a woman had to preserve her "virtue", a man, "sanity." So the whole field of greater reality was left to mystics in the East, psychics in the West. Many seekers found safety in societies and secret orders.

Now my brother and I inherited the Norse ability in both the mystic and psychic field. Our family came from the Orkney Islands and was connected with Iceland. We teamed up with Pamela Barclay whom Lawrence married, and she had the same North Scottish heritage. As she pointed out, Orcadians were that bit weirder!

I discovered a way in which I could share my own intuitive experience without being labelled (very) eccentric. It was through inducing trance in others. At first I could only get people into a deep state where they could describe what was happening, but later remember nothing. This to me was wrong. We should be equals in trance with the operator. The companion on Shamanic journeys should direct their own adventures. We all have such free will in every-day living. I give one of my favourite examples.

A Catholic and a Theosophist, Richard, came to me one Good Friday for a trance session. In doing so, he had missed his Catholic ceremony of "Tenebrae", where candles were ritually extinguished to commemorate the crucifixion. At the beginning of his journey I was faced with the tradition that "right" is good; "left," bad. Richard was on a horse, in armour as Crusader. He had to choose between going left, down into darkness, or to go upwards on the right, to the Light. I was aware that most guides would recommend the right-hand Path of Light. But instead I gave no guidance. He had to choose.

He chose the left-hand Path. Down and down he went, past rocky fissures into the depths. And there, in the shadow of a great rock, he came upon a small chapel. He took off his helmet and entered. It was the beginning of the ceremony for Good Friday, "Tenebrae". And he had to kneel throughout until its completion. And so had I . . .

This introduced to me the whole range of reincarnation experiences through trance. I found that the nearest and most real level was that connected with meeting spirits – family, friends, guides. I believe spiritualist mediums should be greatly respected for their moral courage in really helping people in face of unfair prejudice.

The next sphere involves reincarnation experiences in trance, and usually comes through creating a psychic doorway – a mirror – a dark passage. This is consoling for us, to see "Black Holes," mighty or tiny, not as terrifying phenomena, swallowing stars like oysters, but as a honeycomb of connecting passages, leading through vortices to various levels of consciousness.

The highest level in trance comes through the seeker seeing a light, usually in the sky, and gives the traveller enjoyable angelic visitation. Very often the adventurer remembers nothing of this, or translates the narration given in trance to earthly images. Living lights are seen as flowers, a constellation as "cherry tart!"

Suddenly the legend of Freya's "Apples of Heaven", the "Peaches of Immortality" of Kwan Yin, legends of a magical tree bearing celestial fruit come to life. We have within ourselves the tree of life and the fruits are developing within us. In living time all is everywhere and forever – the past is alive and so is the future. It is we who are stuck in Now. We follow one single time-line. But as we evolve, we find we are part of an intricate pattern of resplendent beauty that involves all that is, not a discriminatory selection of the "righteous," nor rejection of anything, we can alchemically restore what is lost.

So we do not have to be imprisoned in time thinking we were Akhenaton, Nefertiti or Cleopatra. We do not have to settle as "Julius Caesars", "Napoleons" or "Mary Queen of Scots." People are deluded, vain nobodies giving themselves status n the next world because they lack it in this one? No. But such dreamers have instead been projected into living dramas created by the Creators for our benefit. We all act in perennial Mysteries. We join Creators when we tell a good story. TV presenters, religious visionaries, a small child describing a dragon – are not liars. They are

Creators. They are giving local colour to the cosmic reality from which they have been projected by the Deities, to find individuality through experience. Boys find nobility as King Arthur or Robin Hood, girls compassion as Kwan Yin – and as we increase in skills we become a Dostoyevsky or a James Joyce. We learn to include the people around us, and rather than in celebrities, see the glory concealed by shabby t-shirts and denims.

Valhalla, home of the Goddess Vala, Queen of Spirits, has plenty of room in her realm, Asgard. We are there already, but have lost our way in many projections in time. But as we make the way of return, let us bring with us tales of glorious adventures, through which we discover our own originality. Being a Creator is hard but worth it.

"The One-Eyed God"

CHAPTER 2: ICELAND
"A POET'S DOWNFALL"

VISITANTS: PATH GUIDE, ELAINE, PRIESTESS OF ALCHEMY. HELPER, AIDEN, PRIEST OF ALCHEMY. DEIRDRE, ORACLE

TEMPLE OF ARTS - ICELAND

AIDEN: It is dramatic to be invited to this extraordinary Temple with a distant view of an erupting volcano. Reminds me of Hawaii. Frey, as Poet and Arcadian, we gather you wish to share your own experiences with us of your Shamanic Awakening.

FREY: Gladly. My Spirit twin, Freya, has counselled it. Everyone in our group needs this Shaman Quest.

ELAINE: What is your quest?

FREY: I had no idea until I reached my goal, and then it was that I lost everything! You shall hear of my downfall. I would like some dramatic music please – Sibelius' Symphony One. Also red and orange colours – we have the necessary lighting – darkness that then gives way to dazzling colours that affect the chakras. I wish to share my misfortune so that you may help – or fall with me.

ELAINE: We'll take the risk. Proceed.

PART ONE: FREY'S NARRATION

CLASH OF MUSIC AND PSYCHEDELIC COLOURS.

In the time of my Arcadian life I had all you could think of that could give happiness. I had adoring parents – some too adoring – a pleasant village with a good view of our volcano and a superb school, modernist system, with plenty of skiing. Indeed, I think it was this addiction to climbing a rocky gorge near there that led to my failure – see it silhouetted against the flames of our volcano? I've been up there many times and always came down elated with mystical visions. So you see I begin where most of you end - with Arcadian Awakening.

I had it all. My twin soul Freya encouraged me, from her world of spirit, to do deeds of daring. The villagers said I had a charmed life. My mother used to call me Pier Gynt (she was Norwegian). I should have heeded this as an unconscious warning.

One snowy night in November, I was late in returning from an expedition gathering firewood in our sled – not I fear drawn by reindeer but by a motor. It was a night full of the incredible Divine Northern Lights – I should have been more careful, as I made my way home, but I had my eyes on the Lights to the left of the crimson flames of our volcano – and fell into a ravine.

From then on my life changed. Some kindly woodsmen found me and took me to a smart hostel much frequented by visitors – nothing mysterious about them. I felt that our volcano and the Lights were wasted on them. They could only talk of their skiing exploits. So I did not accept their offer of a meal, but sat alone. I wished to attune to the mystique of such a night.

However, there was one visitor who excited my curiosity. He appeared to shun friendly attention much as I was doing. He was wrapped in a long black cloak and I could not catch a view of his face, which was shaded by a wide-brimmed black hat. Then he removed the hat to shake off the snow and I was struck by the dignity of his face. It was aloof, suggesting ancient nobility – not usually seen in our democratic Republic. Suddenly he looked at me with the most brilliant gaze. And when I saw he had a black patch over one eye, I knew I was being scrutinized by Odin. For his eye was not human.

In case you don't know, this God, expelled from the Hall of the Gods, Valhalla, wanders around the northern lands in the way the Wandering Jew pursues his solitary course. Only at Christmas does he ride in blue cloak in a sledge drawn by reindeers bringing gifts of healing herbs.

With a slight gesture of his long white hand, he beckoned me to a chair beside him. Like one hypnotised, I obeyed. I could do no other.

"Frey," he said in a deep musical voice, "my old friend! And I see your brilliant sister is with you! What a pleasure!" Here he beckoned to an invisible Presence and indicated another empty chair. "You have come to the crossroads that will determine your life."

"Your sister has made her choice and is with us in the Holy Realm of Valhalla, domain of the Queen of Spirits, Vala. But you have yet to take up the challenge. It is quite a simple choice. You live a dull life as at present. Or you die and enter Valhalla."

Suddenly I felt icy cold, as if death's frozen hand had reached my heart. I began reciting the Lord's Prayer under my breath and some "Hail Marys". I hadn't prayed for years as I deem myself a Norse Pagan. The terrifying thought came to me that this Pagan God was the Devil.

He read my thoughts and smiled kindly. "You are thinking of later Germanic narratives of Us," he said, "as in the libretto of Wagner's "Ring". You think the Gods and Goddesses built a fortress in the sky they named Valhalla, and were defeated by Giants. They were sent forth in the Destruction of the Gods. I am thus The Wanderer."

"Then, it's a lie." I said hopefully. "Only Christian defamation."

"Not at all," said Odin, beckoning a waiter for more beer, which he sipped with evident enjoyment. I accepted his offer of a glass, which I drank in gulps, hoping it might help. It didn't. "At the early stages of our planetary civilization – primitive, though not as primitive as your present evolution – we created a satellite for military purposes – rather the same as your own weapons of mass destruction – you know the sort of thing – you think they keep your people safe from enemies. We weren't physical as you are – we'd reached a more refined level. For instance you see me, but the rest of the people here can't. They see you drinking beer, talking to yourself, facing two empty chairs. Where was I? Oh yes. We had not outgrown having enemies though! We used to career nicely round this sun, between Jupiter and Mars. Now who was to blame I don't know – which warring faction – 'Giants' versus 'Gods'. In a terrific impact with an asteroid we were destroyed. Etherically that is. Our true Spirits naturally continued, having learnt a useful lesson.

"Our 'Valhalla' admittedly was smashed up and is now circling the sun as the asteroid belt. Our planet itself was hurled forth by Gods more powerful than us, into Outer Darkness nearly beyond your solar system. Well, I suppose we had rather interfered with the Divine Planetary Arrangements. The asteroid belt is unstable, bits flying off now and then, and our planet on a huge orbit goes the wrong way round, at an acute angle, against the traffic lights you might say.

"I say, you've spilt your beer. More? No? Cheer up. It's really all wonderful. There are, I admit, plenty of false Valhallas, but the Great Goddess Vala is in charge of the real ones, sanctuaries of Spirits and these are eternal. There are four lower material levels, like Glitnir – all glitter, but the top three realms are eternal. And one of these is Vala's. And I am offering you a chance to reach the true Home of your Spirit where Freya awaits you – with her Apples of Eternity."

I had heard enough. I panicked - I did not want to die and be with Freya. She's more spiritual than me – I saw everything I had once despised, as being infinitely preferable – food, people, my work. So to my shame I rose to my feet and fled – I just looked back once and saw three empty chairs. Only then did I realise that I had lost my chance of eternal life. You are my last hope. Is there a second chance?

PART TWO: ALCHEMICAL RITE
THE WANDERER RETURNS.
"The Goal and the Path are One."

ELAINE: To understand our roots in the past, we need to invoke the Deities of Destiny. Let us seek the Oracle of the Goddess Vala, Queen of Spirits, who dwells in Her Holy Heaven, Valhalla.

AIDEN *(RAISES STAFF)*: Divine Vala, Queen of the Valiant and Defender of the helpless, You who reign in Divine Reality in Heaven while we struggle in dramas on earth, help this man to achieve his Quest to find Eternal Life, the goal of us all.

ORACLE OF THE GODDESS VALA

All that is – is mirrored in one small seed. Those who aim at their own greatness cut at the very roots of the tree Yggdrasil, the immortal ash that is within and without all nature. Men are ever in such a hurry! Sit with me, Frey, on some pleasant grassy slope. Here you may enjoy many lives, and face the fiery heart of a volcano or black depths of a well, yet receive no hurt.

The time has come for humanity to achieve travel in All-Time, All-Space. You long for adventure. So be it! Harken . . . Lost in the icy wastes of a mountain, frozen from all love and joy, is an imprisoned woman. She neither moves nor speaks nor weeps. Her sleep is dreamless as she is caught in No-Thing. My son, rescue this maiden soul, bring her home to Valhalla. But in the attempt you may lose your life.

ELAINE: We give thanks to the Goddess Vala for Her Oracle.

AIDEN *(TO FREY)*: Are you willing to undertake this task though it may lead to your own death?

FREY: I undertake the quest. I have always wondered why young men, including myself, yearly risk our lives trying the impossible – reaching the summit of the Pole Star Rock! It points towards the Pole Star. Warning notices forbid climbers to make the attempt. But as our long winters darken the world, mothers bar the shutters of windows when darkness comes, to stop their young sons seeing the deadly peak. They have heard of a beautiful ice-maiden who dwells there luring would-be lovers to their death. I believe in this legend because I have met Odin's god-like gaze.

ELAINE: You are ready to make the ascent. I shall be your Path Guide. You will not see me – only hear my voice. In trouble you may call upon the Helper, Aiden, who can aid you in this sphere – and the next.

TRANCE JOURNEY

MUSIC. VIOLET AND GREEN LIGHTING.

FREY: How real this snow is! I could forget the Temple . . . just be here in this blinding storm. But I can hear the soft voice of Elaine – I hear the sound of sea birds from their rock nests . . . I am making my way through the lower slopes of the Pole-Star Rock. I make extremely slow progress. I have been here for hours . . . I am exhausted but I shall not turn back . . . Now I am high enough to face the summit itself which blots out the stars. It is like a terrifying cathedral of ancient Giants! But then I see a wraith-like mist of snow crystals that hides the peak, and the Pole Star behind it.

Ah! It is the form of the most exquisite woman I have ever imagined. No. She is no Woman. At last I behold a Goddess! She is far beyond mere earthly woman. She is robed in snow and shines like ice and her head is crowned by the Polar Stars. She looks into my eyes and I am in heaven of ecstasy. I hold out my arms to her, releasing my hold on the rocks – between me and her is an abyss. I can turn back now – or leap over the abyss to bring her escape from this icy hell . . . I can reach her by a rainbow bridge. I make the leap and fall into total darkness.

I must be dead. I have fallen down a well that seems miles deep. I fall through black cold water. * * *

This is ridiculous. I'm back in that ski resort with noisy visitors. Some kindly men have carried me in front of the fire and women chafe my hands and rub my face – and give me brandy. I hear one of them say to the other: "Another of them! Welcome to Spirit World, young man! You've joined the land of the Goddess Vala – you have won the honour of being admitted in Valhalla, for you have died a hero."

I look around me with astonishment. Those who had presented themselves as vulgar visitors on a skiing holiday, gazing at our volcano – are no less than the Norse Gods and Goddesses! What I took to be a convivial bartender is the mighty Thor. Two or three Valas, co-workers with Vala, are indulging in intellectual discussion with Logi, who is explaining his use of magnetism for his use in their space travel.

Two other Valas are tending to my needs. One of them says to another: "He's really had an easy transition. Violent deaths are often less traumatic than slow dissolution. That's why adventurers are apt to end up here. Vala's Hall is for active service within the Land of Asgard." She addressed me. "We Valas like to help those who face initiatory death. It can be quite a shock."

I look around for help. How about Aiden? I hear his voice very distantly: "You already had a Guide but rejected Him as the Devil! Look for a patch over one eye!" I look round. And there, sitting at a table is Odin! Curious - for a moment he reminds me of my old School Master – the one who annoyed me by saying I was spoilt. At first I could not see his companion. She has her back to me. Then Odin beckons to a vacant chair, and I sit down.

"This is delightful," he says smiling. "It's so pleasant to have Freya with us!"

Then I can see the woman now that she has pushed back her woolly cap to shake off the snow. She looks into my eyes. She is the Icy Goddess of the Pole-Star. I am totally taken aback . . .

She laughs and says: "Frey, answer me this riddle. 'What is it that dwells on the peaks, is lost in the abyss and sits all the while in the tavern in Spirit World'?"

I cannot answer. She replies: "The Golden Apple of Eternity is within Goddess and wanderers, earth humans and spirits. Frey, you are still alive in a physical body and so am I. And there is much work to be done. Who knows? We may meet." * * *

END OF TRANCE.

FREY COMES BACK FROM TRANCE IN ECSTATIC STATE. HE PUTS IT DOWN TO HAVING FOUND VALHALLA. BUT AIDEN COMMENTS THAT HIS TWIN FREYA HAS SOMETHING TO DO WITH IT! IT SHOULD BE INTERESTING TO MEET HER. REPORTS ARE SHARED. THOUGHTS OF HOPE AND COURAGE ARE SENT FORTH.

End of Rite.

A HAPPY FEW DAYS ARE ENJOYED BY THE GROUP, INCLUDING A TRIP TO THE VOLCANO BUT NOT TOO NEAR, DELIGHTFUL THOUGH VALHALLA SOUNDS.

Orcadian Poem by Olivia to the Valhalla motif by Wagner

Love shines like gold in Holy Vala's Hall
Where dwell the Gods and Goddesses in bliss.
There grows the Tree of Life above the Well of Truth.

Sun's Apples gleam in Freya's leafy groves,
Celestial food that brings eternal life.
A rainbow forms an arch
Uniting Heaven and Earth.

Birds call their song of hope to Wandering Souls,
Pilgrims in search of their lost Heaven.
"Within the Mother's Home
Lies hidden the Source of Life."

"The Blue Heaven"

INTRODUCTION TO CHAPTER 3
"THE MAGIC WOOD."

When I was about five years old my sister Barbara, three years older, brought me every night to Fairyland. We were sleeping in the night-nursery of "Hatherlow," in Reigate, in South England. It was a respectable, quiet environment, a gentle preface to my stormy transition to a haunted Irish castle. But my sister's imagination prepared me for anything I might encounter later. She had me screaming in terror by night at "The Boiled Owl and the Guinea Pig." When frequent thunderstorms raged, she explained it was a naughty boy stamping on his nursery floor, and the lightning was his wild hair.

This took place in our nursery. But it was her introduction to me of a land outside the nursery that brought magic and the Goddess into my orthodox suburban existence. For when we were tucked up in our bedroom, Nanny drew the blind. In those days we were expected to lie in total darkness. So she drew down an indigo coloured blind to remove any light. However, she believed in some fresh air, and so she pricked holes all over the blind.

It was those constellations of brilliant dots amidst a streaky blue-green blind that brought me to another and more wonderful world outside the window. The dark blind was a pretence hiding a dark wood with high straight trees. They made a barrier through which we had to find our way to reach Fairyland. We could see the sparkling lights of this land beyond the wood, if only we could reach it.

I was never afraid of the wood. It was so exciting to find my way through the trees, and seeing the lights grow larger and larger. Finally we would reach Fairyland! It was a beautiful and happy land ruled by no less than Queen Jupiter. We never spoke of this place – which was wise. We might have been told it did not exist – or worse, turned into a pretty story suitable for children. I learnt early in life that when you have something precious it is best not to talk of it, except to real friends.

My father introduced me to another sort of magic by playing the piano. This was what I liked best in life. I enjoyed this music during our stay in Reigate – while I was from five to eight years old. But my magical experience of Wagner's "Ring" saga was no more nor less than I receive now at 94! I saw the story in my mind's eye – Brynhilde sent to sleep and Valhalla and river maidens. I was able to visualise Wotan as somebody quite different that I remembered seeing bending over my pram, surrounded by blue light. He appeared when I was 3 months old. I give an account of my own early enjoyment of the magical realm to share the knowledge that it is real.

I was pleased when someone said after a recent Fellowship celebration: "The Priestesses of Isis have smiles on their faces!" I always give trance adventures, whatever the ceremony, because it helps people to find their own personal path. I am careful to leave vision as much as I can to each participant's own awareness. Thus people find their own voice, artistic gifts, and particular vocation.

The twentieth century was dominated by abstract ideals, the concept of the nation, the group and "the masses". Individuality was denigrated. Religion was becoming de-personalised, spiritual, abstract. I was meant to be delighted at the prospect of "becoming a dewdrop absorbed into the shining sea." Why? People had to force themselves to be One with everyone, whether they liked them or not.

It struck me that it was like a process endured by myself when a hygienic friend had the castle "industrially cleaned." It was left smelling like a laboratory, each room and cushion having lost the smell of wood, fabric, scents – one man who had had "a make-over" said that he was so hygienic he could only attract a cabbage moth.

There was once a well-meaning endeavour to "clean up" the Fellowship of Isis by a well-wisher. My brother and I were presented with a lengthy questionnaire to be submitted to all would-be members. We were assured it was used by some of the best Spiritual Orders. Among the queries given were "Have you been in prison?" "Are you an alcoholic?" "Do you use drugs?" "Are you homosexual or lesbian?" "Are you handicapped in your spine?" I was told that one's psychic energy might flow crookedly. I pointed out that electric cables were pliable. "Have you had a nervous breakdown?" Did they refer to "occult blow-outs"? Usual risks to be accepted. If you ticked a "Yes", your application to FOI was to be rejected.

I pointed out that anyone wishing to join, yet having a "Yes" answer, would obviously lie. In any case I thanked the sender for the offer of help but declined the list for the Fellowship of Isis. Our membership would drop dramatically. We had a habit of telling the truth. "Yes" replies would abound. We would not be spiritually cleansed by immersion in a "Shining Sea".

Nothing is more reassuring to our rulers than people aiming to be dewdrops falling into the shining sea. Such folk could be of no possible danger of interfering in politics. They aim to sit quietly on their behinds, possibly in the lotus position if they can achieve that – and shut up.

There is truth in the axiom "For evil to prevail it only takes good people to do nothing." And nobody does nothing better than the three Wise Masters who see no evil, hear no evil, speak no evil. "Cover up" is the golden rule.

What we are being guided to do is to hand over our individual souls into the charge of some Religion, Order or Ideology. We are told we have souls that need saving. The non-believers say we haven't got any. Having surrendered our souls into the custody of a Faith, we are told we will achieve Enlightenment. We are usually asked to pay quite a bit as Enlightenment can cost a lot, like an electricity bill. If we run out of our subscription, the course may stop until we pay up. In the past we gave up our land, even our country, to the religion in power. Now we do it by email.

How on earth or heaven, I asked Isis, can we avoid this carry-on in the Fellowship of Isis?

I received Guidance from Isis. Let us continue with the basic guide-lines as set forth in our F.O.I. Manifesto. Membership is free. People can leave us without question. Charges may be made for books and courses. Every Centre has honour for each member, treated on equal terms. Honour is also given all human-beings and for animals and all creatures. When we awaken into Divine Reality we shall find our lost Heaven has been here all the time! The Truth is only hidden so that we may learn how to draw the Veil from Isis that we may see Her Face.

CHAPTER 3: HAWAII:
"THE SORROWFUL VICTIM."
"THE TYRANT AND THE VICTIM CONTAIN EACH OTHER."

VISITANTS: PATH GUIDE, AIDEN, PRIEST OF ALCHEMY. HELPER, ELAINE, PRIESTESS OF ALCHEMY. DEIRDRE OF THE VISIONS.

TEMPLE OF ARTS - ISLAND OF KAUAI, HAWAII

AIDEN: We are grateful to you, Uri, for inviting Elaine, Deidre and myself to this lovely spiritual centre in this island of Kauai. Elaine, Deirdre, and I feel a strange premonition of great events here. It is no ordinary place.

URI: You have divined well my predicament. This island is the birthplace of us all, born of the Goddess Marama of Dark Space. She is the Mother of the Goddess Haumea, "the Warm Pillar of Fire" within the earth: Mother of the dark oceans of space. It is here that the present human race burst forth from the darkness through a cleft in the Mountain of Birth, Anahola.

DEIRDRE: Indeed, you did show it to us as we drove by. I received a mysterious vision of the future, and would like to return there. I asked in my mind as we drove by: "When will it happen?" And the reply was: "Sooner than you expect!" Yet I don't know what "it" is, or what I expect! I therefore would like to receive the Oracle of the Goddess Haumea. I know that in her "Big Island" is the Tree of Life, with each of us one of Her divine leaves.

URI: Let us pray for Her Oracle. It may help me in my misfortunes.

ALL WEAR ROBES RELATING TO THE SACRED ELEMENTS.

AIDEN *(INVOKES)***:** Come to us, Haumea.

ORACLE OF THE GODDESS HAUMEA

My body is the stem of the Tree of Life growing through this holy earth; my arms are the branches animating sacred centres in each land; my roots are within the womb of Our Mother Marama, and She rejoices to see Her children reach out to the encircling stars in the void of Space. Dearest child

Uri, to attain Heaven, the floating Isles of Kano, you need to pass three voids where your Lower, Middle and Higher Selves are. You need to reconcile all three Selves, so that the sap of my Tree of Life, Mana, may arise through the tree within your body. Otherwise you will be as a withered branch, bringing your sorrows to all you meet.

ELAINE: We give thanks to the Goddess Haumea for Her Oracle.

DEIRDRE: Her presence was very strong. Allow me to lie down and recover.

AIDEN: Uri, She speaks of your sorrows, your longing for the Hidden Islands of Kano, and your failure. Will you tell us about it? We shall listen but not burden you with advice!

PART ONE: NARRATION

URI: I was born on the Big Island of volcanoes. My mother said that my twin brother Eri and I came as lava flowed near our home.

No twins could have been more unlike! My brother Eri was a smiling baby, loved by all! He had a cheerful disposition and enjoyed being cuddled even by strangers – whereas I would scream if anyone touched me. They said I was a plain child, but hoped I would grow out of it . . . I didn't. My mother would look at me and say that my looks were not on her side of the family. If I complained, she would pinch me or slap me hard. She never hit my brother.

My father was proud to have a son, and taught him to sail in our canoe before he could walk. He left me to be cared for by my mother. Once when I complained that she hit me, he replied: "You should obey your mother given to you by the Gods. You will learn to be a true, loving and obedient woman, despite your lack of beauty, which is not your fault."

So I grew up hating my mother beyond any words. I used to day-dream of a kind old woman in our village coming to me one morning to wake me up. "Little Uri," she would say: "I have very sad news for you. Your mother and father were both drowned in their canoe hit by a giant wave. Only your little brother is still alive. You are an orphan." In these day-dreams I never killed Eri. He was always nice to me. He would tell me not to mind what people said or did. He didn't. But then they only did nice things to him and nasty things to me.

However, things suddenly changed when I became a woman. I wore lovely garlands for my hair, which was long and wavy, and I dyed my robes in beautiful sea colours. And a fine young man courted me, and I was very happy.

But one terrible day I heard him making fun of me to a pretty but poor girl of our village. "All this finery," he said, "is like a black bird in borrowed plumage. But her father has wealth so I shall marry her. But I'll never desert you, and I'll give you beautiful presents." And they both laughed.

I was enraged. My mother's devilish temper broke out and I cursed them both. But because of that I had a frightful punishment from the Gods.

I had not realised that the young man was a sorcerer who worshipped a God who had killed his wife. He came to me one nightfall with a cruel smile. He held a package wrapped up in brown cloth.

"Open it, Uri," he said. "It is my farewell gift to you, in gratitude for all you have done for me."

I opened the package. Inside was a curious necklace. It was made of large black nuts or roots. "This, dear Uri," he said, "is the Necklace of Death. While it lasts it will bring about your lingering death. I see what is in your mind. If you dare to cut it, you will die at once. So this is truly a farewell gift." And with this he darted away like a black shadow.

From then on my life changed. I became religious, hoping to break the spell. Eri suggested I just cut the necklace and chuck it into the sea. He would. The man was just angry because he thought I led him on, to hope for a rich marriage. He was too stupid to know that I had fallen in love with him.

So, on another island, I joined a spiritual group. The teachers taught enlightenment through soul saving. They welcomed me, and the Holy High Priest said he would deal with the necklace of death. By saving my soul, I would be free from all evil. So he brought a beautiful alabaster jar, and said I was to breathe into it. So I was giving my soul into his safe keeping. When my soul was cleansed he would release it into their Sacred Pool, to join the rest of the redeemed. Ardently I breathed my soul into the jar and the Priest sealed it with a magical secret sign.

So I joined the Brotherhood, with the permission of my father, a trustee of the Order. I wondered where his soul was in the rows of jars in the Sanctuary, but the High Priest said my father was not ready for Initiation, being too much immersed in material affairs.

The auspicious day dawned when we all assembled round the Sacred Pool. There were four successful candidates before me, who gave testimony of their spiritual experiences. Their jars were opened and the new Initiates had the privilege of passing through a Moon doorway to receive further enlightenment.

Oh my dear friends, how fastly my heart beat, my eyes filled with tears as the seal on my jar was broken. I had left my heartless home, I had given up my lover and now I would receive my reward.

Nothing happened. The jar was held upside down, and the High Priest declared my soul was now purified and luminous and ready for further Initiation. All applauded. I was now to give my Testimony.

But I burst into tears. I could not tell lies and tell them all I had attained Illumination like the others. I cried out: "I am unworthy. I am not blessed. I am not enlightened." And I ran away. I took shelter with the kind old woman in our village and I did washing to pay for my keep. I had disgraced my father and my family. I was a failed candidate, a spoiled Novice, so I was fit for nothing. I've lost my soul . . .

Then I heard of your Society, and you brought me hope as I followed your ideas on the World Wide Web in our village library. You are my only hope. Can you find my soul and bring me to the floating isles of Kano?

AIDEN: Your story has deeply moved us. We will try. . .

PART TWO: ALCHEMICAL RITE
REVELATION OF THE ISLES OF KANO.
"DO NOT BE DECEIVED BY THE MASK."

TEMPLE OF ALCHEMY – KAUAI

DEIRDRE: You are welcome to our trance session, Uri. Your aura is filled with turquoise blue, the colour of hope. Are you willing to enter into trance?

URI: I am filled with longing. It is my last chance to rescue my lost soul. I agree.

AIDEN: Please lie down upon this couch, and close your eyes so that you may see the other land. *** If you feel you need help, call upon Elaine. This is your time to trust in the Goddess Haumea who honoured you with Her Oracle. *** You find yourself in the Land of the Rainbow that lies in an arch about the three Voids. Each void has hidden the Zones of Lower, Middle and Higher Selves. Only in harmonizing these three can you obtain the flow of immortal Life, Mana, that feeds your soul. *** Where are you? Tell us what befalls you.

TRANCE JOURNEY

URI: How strange this place is - there are shadows of many-coloured islands floating on clouds. I am drawn to one land which reminds me of somewhere . . . it enfolds me in a garment of red and brown colours. . .

Oh no! I am back in my home that I abandoned so long ago. I wonder why? My brother Eri appears in the doorway and he says to me that it is where our mother lies in pain, dying. I say "But Eri, this is not her grand house. It is a small hut, shabby and poor!" Eri tells me that my father divorced her some years ago for violent behaviour. He has taken another wife. "The only person who dares come near her in her fits of rage is a good old woman, once a friend of yours. She looks after her but cannot get anyone else for my mother flares up like a dormant volcano!"

Like a flash I become her child suffering again her harsh treatment. I remember her preference for my brother, her contempt for my looks, my words. Now she is properly punished! The Gods are just. But it is strange – I get no happiness from this revenge. Instead, I feel over-whelming pity, not because my mother does not deserve her misfortune, but because she does!

I visit her couch and bend over her. She gazes at me malevolently, her old dislike the same as ever. But I take no notice. I make her room cheerful with flowers and cook her favourite dish, beyond the skill of the old woman. I arrange for proper care for her as I get money from my father.

It is extraordinary – but I feel completely happy! All the thoughts of hatred have vanished. Please explain this Elaine!

ELAINE: Uri, listen if you can to the words of a Dream-worker, one who helps those in confusion.

URI: Yes . . . I hear words in a very gentle boy's voice. "Uri, it is not for you to force your mother to improve! This is for her and only her. All you can do is to offer help. But by doing the reverse of her cruel deeds, by caring for her with love, you have redressed the Balance of Divine Energy! So golden Mana is flowing through your heart. Therefore your mother has helped you despite herself! You have learnt to use your Lower Self, transforming your anger (so like your mother's) into loving energy. You have attained the Initiation of Huna of the Lower Zone."

Now I understand! You can only transform evil into good by balancing it with its opposite. For good is real, and evil is only a passing shadow that vanishes when the truth is seen. I am so happy I could stay here! This is an Island of Kano warmed by the heart's love of Haumea. * * *

But even as I feel this heavenly rapture – there is a frightening change. I am once more in the evil presence of the sorcerer who gave me the Necklace of Death.

"Uri, you have not escaped me!" He says. "You rejected my offer of marriage simply because I laughed at you! I was pleasing a girl I liked, and I wished to keep her. All men do this. But you cursed me and the curse remains." He is holding the terrifying necklace. Now it all comes back to me. I was incensed with rage when I heard him mock me to the girl. So I cursed them with the bite of a shark that leaves blood on the surface of the waters. I fall on my knees.

"Forgive me," I call. "I withdraw the curse of the shark. I will accept your gift of the Necklace of Death as retribution. Only then can I be happy in Spirit realm!"

But suddenly he burst out laughing! He is a God! He says: "Know me for the God Lono. We both have hot tempers. Because you have renounced your curse, see that the Necklace of Death is truly the Rainbow Necklace of the Middle Island of Kano! You have redeemed your Middle Self. Accept this gift!" He offers me the Necklace, not now of Death but of Rainbow Jewels.

This floating Blue Isle of Kano is indescribably beautiful with a thousand many-coloured birds singing in fruit-laden trees. I would stay here for ever – but there is a sudden storm * * * and a tsunami.

To my horror I see my brother Eri's canoe in danger from a giant wave. I rush to his rescue. He puts his arms round my neck as I carry him swiftly to high ground beyond the waves. I intend to take him with me to a fisherman's cottage, but he says "No, no, Uri. They are waiting for you at the Temple high upon this hill. I shall sail far away to the Western Ocean."

My heart sinks. I wish to stay with Eri and not again to face the High White Elders. But I must face them and my father once again. So with slow steps I mount the platform and enter the Temple.

It is exactly the same as before, but the successful candidates are absent, I suppose learning the Mysteries. My father is present beside the High Priest.

To my astonishment the High Priest says: "Uri, you are the only successful candidate at our previous ceremony! The others failed and have returned to junior school." "How can this be?" I ask. "I was unworthy . . ."

The High Priestess smiles. "My dear daughter, you were the only candidate who told the truth!"

The High Priest explains. "All of you thought that you had given your souls as breaths into jars in this Temple. Here was your ignorance. You should have known that your essence – your souls, come from the Great Mother, and so only belong to each one of you. We teach you to discover your true selves within you!"

The High Priestess says: "We, whom you call the Gods, enlighten humanity through Dream Zones. All that you experience on earth is part of dramas you weave yourselves, inspired by our Dream-Walkers, the Aumakuas. We awaken Mana, the sap from Haumea's Tree of Life. It is the will of the Mothers that you should grow strong and true and bring love and joy to all . . ."

I can see the Aumakuas. They are shining and kindly Spirits. One places a robe, a blue robe about me, and another places a shining gold crown upon my head. As she does this, I feel a shower of stars descending upon me. I feel Divine Spirits are drawing me to dance with the stars whirling around me in the sacred void of space. I am spreading forth wonder and inspiration to all! I see my Father as a dignified Professor, and my Mother as a Protectress of sea birds, which she always loved. Eri sails far away among the Northern stars. I shall teach Huna, our own path. Yet, we are all together in Spirit. For our own earth is a hidden Isle of Kano. It is there all the time.

END OF TRANCE.

End of Rite.

URI SLOWLY RETURNS FROM TRANCE FEELING BLISSFUL. WE HAVE A FEAST BY THE SEA-SHORE, AND WE ENJOY THE EVENING STARS AS WE SWIM IN THE STILL SEA. WE GIVE THANKS TO THE DEITIES.

Sources: "Oceanic Mythology, The Myths of Polynesia, Micronesia, Melanesia, Australia," and "Myths and Legends of the South Seas", Roslyn Poignant, Hamlyn Pub. "Children of the Rainbow, The Religions, Legends, and Gods of Pre-Christian Hawaii", Leinani Melville, Quest Books. "Mark Twain in Hawaii: Roughing It in the Sandwich Islands, Hawaii in the 1860's," Mutual Publishing, Honolulu.

"Goddess Uta-Ha"

INTRODUCTION TO CHAPTER 4
"THE ENCHANTED DOORWAY."
"THE GREATER COMPREHENDS THE LESSER: THE LESSER IS PART OF THE GREATER."

I expect like so many of you who are beset by a multitude of Causes to protest about, you long for a respite! One is reminded of the words of the Cabalistic "Zohar": *"God did not banish humanity from Paradise. Humanity banished God."* So sometimes, when we are wearied of battling against child abuse, cruelty to animals, destruction of wild-life, we may not fight evil with its own weapons – force, exposure, the Army, the Law – but with good.

I liked the Sermon on the Mount, turning the other cheek, forgiving enemies, but thought it didn't work. Valiantly I maintained my pacifism even in the Battle of Britain when I was a nurse – but later gave it up as the onslaught of exposure of atrocities multiplied. Then we fought factory farming and the wanton destruction of nature, with our pens and voices. I gave up being a vegetarian when I found the origin of apparently innocent food stuffs and chose Organics.

I sided with those New Agers who had a placard conveniently by the front door, blazoned with the brave words "I PROTEST" – leaving a space for the particular evil to be attacked in a demonstration.

But how were we to be happy ourselves? Were we to await death and "Rapture"? Not for Protesters. After death we then had to do Rescue Work, saving souls trapped in various challenging environments once called Hells. Some of us signed the Bodhisattva Oath, electing to stay on in various hells until all beings were saved – rescuing them with the Light. But, as one Teacher said to me: "I'm expected to stay in hell forever – or as long as it takes – but this is not possible. I sit perfectly happily on a sunny day, drinking a glass of beer – next to a man in hell. He is going through the torture of jealousy. I can't help being happy. I'm in Heaven where I sit. He is in the same place but cannot feel the warmth of the sun, hear the laughter of people drinking at little tables, the song of blackbirds, or smell the scent of lime flowers. One is in Heaven. One is in Hell. Each must choose. We can be helped, but truly, we are expected to save ourselves through the way we live."

I did notice that this man, when he sat anywhere, brought serenity with him. Some saw light around him, and shared in the peace and light. He never preached at them but would talk easily if approached.

Here evil was eliminated, not by terrified conspiracy theories, not by moral indignation, protest or violence. Where he lived *was* Heaven.

The secret, I believe, rests in our attitude to time. Forever is now. Our beginning in evolutionary progress is contained in the greater reality of our cosmic origin. Within us we have the seed of immortality – the jewel within the heart of the lotus. Our great adventure is like a traveller, making our way through the beautiful, awe-inspiring infinity growing in wisdom and love. We choose our roles in various lives.

My way is through the extending of my earthly senses to psychic awareness. For me this was the awakening of vision. My gift was developed in group through enhancing eidetic imagery – pictures seen in the mind's eye. I was surprised to see how quickly this happened. I remembered knowing George Russell, the Irish mystic, "AE," and I respected his description of the development of the most advanced mystic experience.

In my case the eidetic imagery started humorously, with cartoon characters, in two dimensions. I remember a canoe full of Native Americans with feathers, capsizing and then swimming ashore. I enjoyed a procession of animals queuing up at a food counter, being served by a lion with a white apron. The colours were extraordinarily brilliant. I felt my invisible teachers were laughing at me in a kindly way.

I was told that the next stage would be a three-dimensional scene, and that I would learn to go into the scene. This was heralded by what was called "beds of tulips", like Muslim designs. But then I got my first realistic picture – a little girl in a red dress, on a balcony of a French chateau. I could enter if I chose but needed to create a doorway to get out again!

My friend Melita Denning and I once enjoyed an aerial trip to Switzerland while sitting in her flat in Hampstead. What we did was to turn on the television and then obliterate the picture, so we just had the electric power which helped. We visited a spiritual centre there, far from the "cuckoo-clock" image of that country.

Clairaudience comes unexpectedly for me but very strong. I think the way this happens is by slowing down thought. My brother, Lawrence, versed in these matters, as was his wife Pamela, said that telepathy came through the stillness between our thoughts. I have experienced telepathy with spirit beings that was as clear as earthly speech.

I notice that many so-called scientific authors have power of the mind – but leave out the heart. For instance I love reading utopian novels by brilliant writers but notice the heartlessness of the so-called supermen held up for admiration. I think this comes because the mind with its logical workings and telepathy of thought needs balancing by empathy. The seat of empathy is not up in the head. It glows in the solar plexus and the womb. It resembles a wild rose which reigns in every heart and grows in the darkness, until it is drawn forth by the descending light.

The two pillars of light and darkness lead to the inner Heaven concealed around us. It is the blending of the two Powers, Truth and Love, that create the cosmos. The Fates weave the shining rays of light and darkness and so produce their work of Art; the tapestry of Creation. Increasingly, as we develop, we join in this weaving and help to create our own destiny. This why we fell from the divine realm of Perfection – in order to find our own way back home, bringing with us what we have gained, our own individual gifts.

CHAPTER 4: UTAH

"TO KNOW YOURSELF YOU NEED TO SEEK THE OTHER; LOOK IN A POOL AND YOU WILL SEE YOUR LOVER."

HOST IN UTAH: LUIS SIVA. VISITANTS: PATH GUIDE, ELAINE, PRIESTESS OF ALCHEMY. HELPER, AIDEN, PRIEST OF ALCHEMY. DEIRDRE OF THE VISIONS.

TEMPLE OF ARTS - UTAH

ELAINE: Thank you, Luis Siva, for inviting us to this wonderful mountain land. I wonder that you need our help so urgently. It is so orderly in your Utah Iseum with its library and computers.

LUIS: And so it was until on a fatal journey I made to my old university last year. My father is part Spanish, part Native American, and is set on my obtaining a Doctorate in comparative religion. I know why. Our family blends three traditions – my mother is Hindu. She has had Puja done for me for my acceptance into our Temple here. It is dedicated to the Deities Kali, Siva and Ganesh . . . Hence my second initiatory name.

AIDEN: This must give you a keen interest in religion.

LUIS: Quite the contrary. It has given me a strong dislike of any sort of faith. I am doing the Doctorate in order to bring scientific rationalism to expose cults and religious dogma. I wish to escape from being confined to any tradition that does not conform to scientific facts. My computer is my best friend.

AIDEN: It is worthy to seek the truth. Facts are the sandaled feet of a statue to Truth. Otherwise religious statues have feet of clay.

ELAINE: Yet feet of clay bring the Deity down to Mother Earth!

DEIRDRE Where the fallen statue lies in the mud, there can be no miracles, and as Prophetess I deal in miracles!

AIDEN: Let us hear your story, and what has happened to destroy your faith in materialist science.

PART ONE: NARRATION

LUIS: A woman. No ordinary woman. She has ruined my life, destroyed my reputation for sanity, by entirely taking over my life – and all for nothing. What is in a name?

ELAINE: How did this happen to you? You seem so level-headed.

LUIS: None more so. Or so I thought. It happened on the plane journey back to my home in Utah. I was sitting with my laptop working out statistics of the number of cults in Utah, compared with those in California – there are less in Utah, but more virulent because they are underground – undermining logic and known scientific facts.

Suddenly there came unexpected turbulence which rocked our plane. One of my papers fluttered to the floor, by the feet of a woman who I now observed was sitting next to me. She bent and picked up the paper. She glanced at it and smiled. I don't know why, but I felt offended; I felt she was laughing at it . . . She looked at me.

I was startled. She had "wall-eyes," one being greenish brown, the other a clear sky blue. Then I felt embarrassed at staring at what was a physical defect. She seemed to reply to my thoughts. "I like having wall-eyes," she said. "It gives me dual perspective – a dialogue between them! I am earthly, and I am spiritual."

I should have been wary of getting into conversation, but she had touched on my determination to find facts about so-called spirituality. I found myself inviting her opinion on my forthcoming thesis. She handed me back my paper, and in so doing, touched my left hand. I felt an electric shock shoot through my body, inducing a feeling of ecstasy. For the rest of the journey I was in heaven. She told me of my own native land as a place of wonder, with soaring mountain ranges with undiscovered gorges, and said that below were underground tunnels and a volcano. I remember she told me she had a woman friend who had shared a course on volcanoes in Hawaii and they sometimes worked together. I wish now I had asked where they both worked. But too soon the flight ended. She drew a handwoven, woollen cloak around her, picked up a Native American bag and that was the last I saw of her.

AIDEN: Didn't you follow, get her name and number on your mobile?

LUIS: Of course, that is what I usually do. But she went so swiftly and I had to get my own suitcase of books from the luggage hall. It took forever. Then I looked for her everywhere in the airport and outside. And from then on I have been obsessed. I must find her. Nothing else matters. My mother says I have been bewitched, and wanted me to be exorcised by a Priest of Kali. But I said that would make it worse! A statue now has the effect of making a fire burn within me. I know now why the words "in love" are used and not "I love." You fall into love for your will-power is gone. Or rather you don't want any cure. You delight in your very anguish.

ELAINE: So what did you do?

LUIS: I broke my father's heart. I burnt all my papers. I gave my friends my laptop. I presented my father with my mobile and I left home for my search. I brought little with me, only the bare necessities. I even gave up my spectacles! Indeed, my eyesight began to improve and I found I could easily tramp fifteen to twenty miles a day.

At first I enquired her name from the Mormons, who were extremely courteous and called me Brother – but even their extensive genealogical library could not help as I had no name for this woman. They showed me hundreds of photos, but no-one was like her. I tried the Freemasons, but their Women's Lodge could not trace her. The Witches could not have been kinder – but found no trace of her in their coven records. The Spiritualists consulted their Guides. However, they declared that they did not give away personal details of anyone. Obviously the lady wished to be incognito. I must respect this.

So I made the decision to seek her where, from her words to me, she might be found. So I made a long trek up a mountain in a snowy range, part of the Rocky Mountains. It was divinely beautiful. I found a small resting place in a hut. At first I was overcome by the magic of stars, glittering in wheeling constellations high above the shining snow of the mountain peaks.

But now I became aware of a new sense that had been growing in me since I had received the "electric-like" shock. It was the sixth sense, which before I had denied. I lay down to sleep wrapped in my sleeping bag, before the embers of a wood fire – when I became aware of ghostly faces. There were a myriad of faces of lonely frozen people who I first assumed had perished in the snow. But I became aware that they were captured by icy-cold thoughts without love or hope. They drew near to me as one of them. Around them were diagrams, geometrical shapes, theorems, schedules, systems and ideologies that had brought atrophy of all feelings. I found myself promising them that I would find the secret name of a woman who would save them. I would return. I left them with hope.

I came down the mountain. Below were underground caves. The moment I rested on my dark way – I saw faces. This time they were as distorted as in medieval paintings of purgatory. They were, I thought trapped in some mining catastrophe – but then I found they had been imprisoned in underground tunnels by the most extreme emotions. They let me feel that I could not know their rage, their desire for revenge, their violence against their enemies. I found myself assuring them that I knew a woman who would rescue them – if only I could find her. I needed her name. When I found her I would return.

I made my way back to a motor-way, more dead than alive. Then, at a wayside café, I met a Priestess of Isis who told me of your fellowship. She advised me to write to you. I had no computer so I wrote a long-hand letter. And here you are! You are my last hope. Life without this woman is meaningless.

AIDEN: Your whole desire is to find love?

LUIS: I seem to have changed. Now I really want to help those spirits whom I never believed in! Their state is infinitely worse than mine. Something must be done and I want to do it with the woman's help.

ELAINE: We all agree with this move – so we will try - but only if the woman is willing to reveal herself.

PART TWO: ALCHEMICAL RITE
THE HEAVEN OF THE HIDDEN GODDESS
"THE KNOWN IS OUR PAST.
THE UNKNOWN IS OUR FUTURE."

TEMPLE OF ALCHEMY – UTAH

DEIRDRE: It is customary for us to invite the Oracle from the Goddess presiding over the Rite. However, we are impeded here by the fact that although we know what the Deity looks like, we do not know Her Name. Last night I asked for the name, and the Goddess told me I could successfully invoke Her by the title she bestowed upon this land "Uta-ha."

ELAINE: Our intention is to receive the Divine Name of the Goddess so that this man may bring help to those entrapped by the Elements of height and depths.

AIDEN *(RAISES STAFF)*: Divine Goddess Uta-ha of this land of mountains and desert, you have appeared to our friend as a Guide. Give us your Oracle that we may know the Divine Purpose of this visitation.

DEIRDRE IN TRANCE.

ORACLE OF THE GODDESS UTA-HA

More and more the clever ones of humanity are obsessed with the acquisition of factual knowledge. They are encouraged by those greedy humans who use this scientific knowledge for the possession of power and wealth.

This accumulation of facts does not bring the wisdom of how to use such knowledge. Thus the planet is in peril.

Humanity is blind, deaf, and insensitive to this glorious earth, which contains other dimensions of endless variety. You sit in your planes and draw down blinds to shut out the light of the heavens. Then you read or use computers. In the planet of the blind it is wise to learn to see with true vision.

This comes from extending your awareness, of a caterpillar on a leaf, a darting fish, the wings of a golden eagle. There is no separation in Divine Reality.

You seek my Name. It is hidden in the riddle of the Sphinx, the smile of a new-born baby, the playfulness of a cat. For Cosmic consciousness is only limited by your ability to enjoy what surrounds you! You will find my Name in works of art, in love of your friends, in widening your experience of Love, Truth and Harmony. The mystery of Name is in sound. Listen. It is the music of the spheres and the song of birds.

AIDEN: We give thanks for this Oracle. *(TO LUIS)* Are you willing to enter trance, which is the realm that blends heaven and earth?

LUIS: I am willing. My mind has brought me nothing to sustain me. My mind has only brought me endless doubt.

TRANCE JOURNEY

LUIS *(IN TRANCE)***:** I find myself contemplating the mighty snow-capped mountain range that I have visited before. Beneath it is the lava tunnel to lower depths. I promised to return, but have nothing to offer . . . Then I hear the sound of drumming. It is enlivening in this vast desert. I approach a small party of students who are having an outdoor drumming session. I ask may I join them. They invite me to sit and share their coffee, and sandwiches now curling up in the heat. I know I am not much older but I feel like an uncle! They are so relaxed. Then a very old woman wearing a long white feather on her head would like to offer a story. She tells a tale while the drummer beats a rhythm. A girl shakes a rattle. "There is a secret sacred Mesa," she intones, "known only to the Elders. Its Gateway is hidden behind a mighty waterfall. The seeker finds it in a cleft in the rock behind the water. Through this is the Heaven of the Hidden Kachina. No man has looked with impiety in her face and lived. One tribe calls her "Pte San Win" – her totem is White Buffalo. She teaches that men and women when in harmony are as the stem and bowl of the holy pipe of peace. Our tribe call Her Woman of the White Mountain. Her hair is as the growing plants and Her cloak is made of rushing waters and black ravines. One eye is that of the sky: the other is the earth. Those men who approach Her with disrespect, die with dishonour."

I cry out: "Oh, tell me Her name."

But when I say this the old woman covers her face with her cloak and the students pack quickly saying the sky is darkening for a storm. I rise to my feet and wonder where I shall take shelter. Then I notice a winding path covered with mosses. I follow it, and soon I am protected from the coming storm by overhanging branches of trees.

Now I hear a roaring which I take to be a tornado and turn to flee. Instead I see a great waterfall, flowing in two streams. One stream is of a dark greenish colour, shaded by the surrounding vegetation – the other is clear white and blue, reflecting the Southern sky . . . I find I can make my way behind the fall of water. I find the cleft in the rock and know that the old woman was a true Elder, and was helping me. I enter and find myself in total darkness.

I make my way guided by a soft green light before me. And easily and naturally I find the land beyond.

"It is so simple and natural!" I hear laughter, and there are the students with their coffee and sandwiches! "We're glad you found your way" says the young drummer. "We often come here, and so do our friends. It's funny though – some people can't get here . . . They say we're making it up. Do stay with us!"

"I'd like to stay here with you, and join your session," I say. "But I promised people to do something and must go on. I have to find the Goddess's Name." The girl with the rattle looks worried. "It's not safe for young men," she says. "You heard the warning of the Elder. Many young men like you have died when they faced the Lady of the White Mountain. She works with her friend, Pele of Hawaii. They make volcanoes as casually as we girls make bread! To them death means nothing. They are immortals. You are not."

But I choose to continue. The beat of the drum is becoming faint and then I hear it no more. Nothing happens. I struggle on and on. But then a tornado strikes. Trees are uprooted and I clutch onto a sapling that has bent to the storm.

Suddenly there is a hush. I feel a sense of extending in space and time. I am above the Americas, and I now am far back in the past. I am flying in some ship, which takes me to the future. I see other ships like comets. Then I become aware that the whole spectacle of our planets circling round our sun is receding into tiny points of light. They are becoming a part of a swirling spiral, turning round the mighty central vortex of our galaxy. Even this recedes and becomes part of a shining divine form. I see this is the naked body of the Goddess. One eye now forms our Milky Way; the other is our sister, the Andromeda Galaxy. The face begins to become clearer, and smaller and smaller. I am gazing into the eyes of the woman in the plane . . .

She smiles kindly. "Of course you can use my Name," she says, "if you can hear it."

As everything becomes a whirling spiral, I hear clear, beautiful notes. And I know the Name.

LUIS REMAINS SILENT FOR SOME TIME. THEN HE SPEAKS QUIETLY.

I remember my commitment to the people trapped in the mountain, and those within the earth . . . I am too weak to travel – but a kindly truck driver comes to my rescue as I sit by the roadside, and he gives me a lift. He says he is going up ten thousand feet into the mountains to deliver stores to a small settlement. Halfway up I recognise where I am, and thank the driver as I get out. I wrap myself in the sleeping bag for warmth in the same place where I rested before. Once more the faces come to me, a multitude, each with a story of how they had been trapped. I hear of ideals betrayed, systems disproved, recognition denied. I do not attempt to clarify theologies, Laws of Nature, mathematical structures and infallible dogmas. Instead I put all my faith in uttering the Name. As I do this, the sonics begin to shake the icy prison – the walls crack and the prisoners are freed!

Heartened and stronger, I now make my way down the lava tunnel to the underworld. Here, above a vortex, ghostly figures surround me with tales of hatred, revenge, ambition and the despair of suicides who now find they cannot die. I do not try to cure jealousy, hatred, violence. Instead, I put all my feelings into uttering the Name. This time the sonic power breaks open the roof of the cavern with a seismic upheaval – daylight pours in, and the prisoners are free. And so am I!

END OF TRANCE.

End of Rite.

LUIS TAKES A LONG TIME TO RECOVER FROM TRANCE. HE SAYS HE WAS TRYING TO REMEMBER THE SPIRITUAL JOY AND LOVE HE HAD FELT. IT COULD NOT BE RECLAIMED BY A COMPUTER . . . HE INTENDS TO DO A COURSE IN DEEP MEDITATION.

Sources: "The Varieties of Religious Experience, A Study In Human Nature," William James, Penguin Classics. "The Candle of Vision." AE (George Russell), Macmillan, London. "A Prisoner in Fairyland," Algernon Blackwood. "The Most Holy Trinosophia", St. Germain, edited by Manley P. Hall, The Philosophical Research Society. "The New Atlantis", Francis Bacon. "Strange News from Another Star," Hermann Hesse.

"Sophia, the Lion and the Rose"

INTRODUCTION TO CHAPTER 5
"WHERE IS BOHEMIA?"
"WHERE YOUR HEART IS, THERE IS HOME."

Encouraged by my defusing the terror of the Four Horsemen of the Apocalypse, by introducing the "Four Sacred Donkeys of the Zodiac," I began noticing other creatures unfairly despised or feared by our aggressive humanity. For instance, wolves are unfairly thought of in a creepy way. I made friends with a wolf in Arizona and was photographed with her in my bed. Her eyes shone like lamps. Far away in Ireland, when I was having bother psychically, this Wolf projected in my room and asked: "Are you all right?" The translator in the brain turned this query into English. I said: "Thank you for asking. I'm fine!" In America one says that. In Ireland with an Irish wolf I would have said: "Not so bad."

Wolves are our Robertson protectors, shown as such in our Coat of Arms. But what about our treatment of their descendents, dogs? They get kindness, even compassion, as we train them to be good to children, severe to thieves, and dangerous to our enemies. But though in England dogs are permitted to lie on sofas and beds – they lack dignified status. Cats were Goddesses in Egypt, and still keep their pride. Pekinese were Royal in old China. But they have been bred to be tame miniature lions, like Japanese Bonsai mini-trees. Like dogs we train them as we choose.

The lack of Divinity in dogs was brought home to me in a Bohemian restaurant in Arizona. I saw on one vast wall, a magnificent painting of the Last Supper as recorded by Leonardo da Vinci. But then I looked closer with astonishment Christ presided benignly over the supper as a fox-terrier. On his chest reclined a beautiful Afghan dog, with long, blonde ringlets. The Apostles were depicted as various breeds including a dachshund. On the table were cups including the Holy Grael, I presumed.

I was so delighted with the picture that someone suggested I should get a coloured photograph to bring back to Ireland. But already trouble was brewing! A man objected, saying the Afghan with ringlets was Mary Magdalene, rather than the Beloved John. "I must be tactful," I said, "bringing a photo. They are Catholics and Protestants in Ireland. They would think I was insulting their faith. Some call dogs 'Brute Beasts'." A friend suggested hopefully I might get shot! "No," I said. "We are not that religious nowadays – except in certain counties . . . But I would not dream of showing saints as dogs."

However, the honour of dogs has been restored! I was explaining to a friend how the Jackal God Anubis came to our temple. She asked: "The Jackal-headed Anubis with a man's body?" "No", I replied, "An animal Jackal, seated on a throne. He is a God, Son of the Goddess Nephthys and the God Osiris."

A Priestess gave me an old Egyptian appliquéd wall hanging of the Goddess Muth, with Anubis on his throne below. I duly put this in our Temple. That night I was awakened by the sound of a rumpus in the Temple. I projected psychically down four flights of stairs to the Temple, and found our orange cat Honey-Howler in a mock battle with what I thought was a black dachshund. But he had long upstanding ears and long legs. He jumped up into my arms and licked my face! I wiped it off, and he tentatively licked me again. It was Anubis!

So now in our Cave of the Mothers, Anubis is depicted as a Jackal on his throne, on the altar with a painting of Isis and Osiris, rising into the starry sky. For Anubis is Guide to the constellation of Orion and the Sirius star of Isis. He can also be our Guide so that we too may know our own immortality.

Where can the eccentric, rejected and the abused find their true home, where they are accepted with respect and love? Where else, but Bohemia?

I found the perfect answer in Elizabeth, Queen of Bohemia herself. Shakespeare wrote her story in "The Tempest." She was Miranda, the Philosopher Prospero her father. The romantic lover, Ferdinand, found her in a startling island with faeries and a witch, and other unusual characters. Strangely Elizabeth's own real life story came some years later. Her romantic Rosicrucian initiation ended with a tempest.

The idealistic pair, the Winter King and Queen of Bohemia – came, one should think, from some distant ideal planet – brought through initiations of the Rosicrucian enlightenment. They would not have been surprised by seeming disaster. To lose their kingdom to enemies who laughed at them – would be a Test. Frederick was killed in battle, and Elizabeth was exiled in the Haag in Holland.

Ah – but this is what interests me. From there she created the mythic Bohemia that spread throughout the world. It flourishes in Manhattan, Chelsea, Moscow, Tokyo – wherever Utopia is sought for, not through Empire or violent revolution, but through Art and Nature.

People flocked to her court of every kind of unusual characters – "weird", animal-lovers, pantheists, performers, pagans, anyone with originality. They had been driven out of Bohemia itself, and any land where people who had creative originality were persecuted or laughed at. Elizabeth surrounded herself with every sort of animal and bird, including a monkey which must have removed any of that pomposity associated with courts. Elizabeth deserved her title of Queen of Hearts and Shakespeare's Miranda.

Yes, I have been happy in Bohemia in France, Germany, Sweden, Japan, Hawaii, Yucatan and in eight states in the United States. I am writing this in our Irish Bohemia, with a giant black mountain dog, a miniature dachshund, two pot-bellied black pigs, white, black and orange cats – a varied family and friends. We welcome Spirit friends, usually discouraged in other old castles. Like Kipling's Irish Kim, we are friends to all the world.

CHAPTER 5: BOHEMIA

"TO LIGHT THE FLAME WITHIN WE NEED A SPARK FROM THE STARS."

HOST IN BOHEMIA, PART NOW OF A MODERN STATE: SOPHIA DOROTHEA. VISITANTS: PATH GUIDE, AIDEN, PRIEST OF ALCHEMY. HELPER, ELAINE, PRIESTESS OF ALCHEMY. DEIRDRE OF THE VISIONS, ORACLE.

TEMPLE OF ARTS THE BOHEMIAN WOODS

AIDEN: We are fascinated, Sophia, that historical Bohemia still exists within this highly technical state! I wish you hadn't lost your name "Bohemia" which everyone in the world has heard of! "La Boheme" is the most performed of all operas.

SOPHIA: That is not all we have lost. A whole magical tradition has dissipated, only kept alive in various esoteric societies, unknown to the world. I cannot tell you how many of such Orders I have joined – to no avail. The true mystery of "Rosa Alchemica" is kept from me. I am in despair.

ELAINE: Dear Sophia, Take Heart! When the soul is in despair, then the Goddess manifests in all Her Light. Let us invoke the golden beauty of the Goddess Vesta of the Eternal Flame!

DEIRDRE: Already I feel the Presence of Vesta. This is a secret holy place revered in ancient times by the Goddess of the Melusina solar flow of Divine Life.

AIDEN *(RAISES STAFF)*: Holy Goddess Vesta, invisible to the eye of the profane, glorious in beauty to those who seek you, come among us to fill our emptiness!

ORACLE OF THE GODDESS VESTA

You call upon that which you have already! I speak through this visionary, yet I also come to you in silence, in darkness, when you are most in need. For I am the Divine Love that burns in the heart of all beings born of the

Mother. And all are so born but are taught to ignore their own Divine nature. Ambitious teachers are possessed by a longing to create, to rule, to possess the souls of their followers. But when divine power is blocked, power diminishes, bringing despair. Then I come. But I must be sought for. It is your will which draws you to my will, in freedom. Unity with my eternal flame from the holy darkness brings you rebirth into your greater Being. Now feel my Presence of Light through your bodies! I come from below with Love, and from above as Wisdom. Where these meet, flowers the Mystic Rose. You are no longer alone. My Rose joins heart to heart with joy, and wisdom brings harmony.

ELAINE: We give thanks to the Goddess Vesta for Her Oracle.

AIDEN: It is customary for us to hear in truth why we have been invited to this beautiful Temple hidden in a wood that has just lost its protective covering of snow. We expect your narration.

THE NARRATION

SOPHIA: My soul is dry. I ask you to play some music of our Nature composers, Smetana, Dvorak and Sibelius for the trance.

My upbringing had no such romantic emphasis. My mother died giving me birth, and my father named me Sophia Dorothea after an ancestress who had a disastrous love affair. He said from this misfortune I should learn wisdom from my name Sophia – not the name of any Goddess or Saint, but of abstract Wisdom. So I had the most extraordinary upbringing. My father was a Professor of Astrophysics in our local University, and from the age of five I was introduced to spiral galaxies, "Black Holes," and the folly of astrology. He was an F.R.A.S. My father always got irritated when the words "Astronomy" and "Astrology" were linked. I had no Guardian Angel, as my father explained that to have wings an angel would need a gigantic chest bone to support them. Actually, he gave the number in feet.

His faith lay in the immutable Laws of Physics. Saints could not levitate against the law of gravity – but he had to reconcile Newton and Einstein. One's only hope of soul survival, after death, lay in Samuel Butler's offer of vicarious existence. One lived on in people's memory. This did not appeal to me. Ghosts and such phenomena were due to some energy not yet understood – I gather a sort of television that recorded the passing show.

So I had no soul, nor had anyone else. We did or could have a vague God as an hypothesis.

But it was my moral education that he centred on, as I was his only child, and I suppose he loved me, though he never mentioned this. He would give me little lessons as to the proper reaction I should display to show forth my correct attitude. He was by profession a distinguished engineer, and had an immense admiration for the Golden Gate Bridge in San Francisco.

I was often told to imagine a bone-idle and drunken illegal immigrant lying by the bridge in a stupor. I held a live bomb. I had the choice. Either I should blow up the useless drunk – or the Golden Gate Bridge! And I invariably gave the wrong answer. I insisted on blowing up the Bridge.

Another query was often repeated. This concerned the Louvre in Paris with its painting of Leonardo's Mona Lisa and other great works. Again I held a live bomb. I was either to blow up The Louvre – or a beggar boy sitting outside, cap for coins, busily defiling the pavement with graffiti of an objectionable sort. Once more I disappointed my father – I blew up the Louvre. Indeed, I animated both tramp and beggar into lively friends! So you can understand that having gained my degree in University to please him, I then rebelled against my father's philosophy of the Greater Good – called Fascist, in going against the so-called laws of nature. I joined a group of drop-outs. Among these rebels I found a Lover.

At first he seemed ideal. He had long hair, was unshaved. He taught our group that we should do just what we wanted to. We should make love how and where we chose. He encouraged violent revolution – usually in the form of protests in foreign countries where we could make the most upheaval.

However, things did not go well with our relationship. As I was told I had total control of love making, I refused. I think it was his habit of swallowing poached eggs whole. Like all of our group he had to have his own way. We were like angels when all went well – but demons if we were "crossed".

When I rejected the Lover he suddenly showed another side to his character. Proudly he told me he was "vengeful." I soon got to know what that meant. He wished to have his revenge on his parents for being capitalists. He wished to punish the authorities for banning drugs. And above all he wished to punish anyone for offending his vanity. I realised that he was indeed a Lover: A lover of himself.

With difficulty I extricated myself from his group. But now I was completely alone. I was used to being instructed. I had learnt so much from my father that I had a Double First Degree in Physics and Mathematics in our University. And through the riotous years with the Lover and his eccentric friends I had made a reputation as a film maker. I even have my own television programme.

ELAINE: Then you seem to have all you need. You were a follower of Masters – Luciferian of heights and Satanic of the depths – and you come out looking very elegant and competent. Why do you need the Fellowship of Isis?

SOPHIA: You see my persona. I preside over programmes with the knowledge taught from my father, and the passionate feelings introduced by the Lover. But this learning and this passion, are not part of my real self! I feel I am becoming less and less real the more successful I become. My true self has become a shadow banished by a false Sophia forged by teachers.

So I hope to find myself. I do remember being a happy baby – before my education. I've had glimpses through music and friendship. But what finally terrified me was what happened to my father and the Lover. I have never told anyone this. But I must. My father has lapsed into deep "clinical melancholia." He is shut in an icy realm where he is not aware of warmth, friends, even animals.

I did not recognise the Lover when I visited him in a basement flat in a rough part of his town. He was living in a secret world induced by hard drugs. He says he is in an underworld with blazing fires and many people – not beings I would care to meet, judging from his description. He had been so much in control of his followers – but now is dependent on outside help. He certainly needs it, but not from those to whom he turns, who are as ill as he is.

And I cannot help either him or my father. They have taken away my own self with their projections of what they wanted me to be. Perhaps they did love me as they thought I was . . . Then I met one of your members, a Priest of Isis, who said that I had given all I had to these two men and now I was empty of the life flow of the Goddess. They could not help me. Nor can I help them. So I turn to you.

PART TWO: ALCHEMICAL RITE
THE LAND OF MACARIA OF THE MYSTIC ROSE.
"TRUTH RULES ALL: LOVE IS WITHIN ALL."

HOLY TEMPLE OF ISIS OF THE VESTAL FLAME - BOHEMIA

AIDEN: We are in your Holy Temple of Isis of the Vestal Flame. For us to help you, we have invoked the Goddess Vesta. She has been with you during your Temple sleep during the night. Are you willing to face the maze that brings the Heart's Desire? It is an ordeal of the soul.

SOPHIA: It is an Initiation that I have been searching for all my life. I am practiced in soul journeys. I am prepared. I have slept with a lighted candle dedicated to Vesta of Enlightenment.

ELAINE: Preparation involves a determination to face the Truth, however painful – the truth facing oneself, without transferring wrong to others! I am here as Helper.

TRANCE JOURNEY

SOPHIA LIES ON A COUCH, ARMS FOLDED, EYES SHUT. SHE IS HERSELF ENTERING TRANCE STATE. SHE GIVES HER REPORT:

The desire of my heart is to find the magical land of Macaria. I have longed to find it since I read of it in Moore's "Utopia" and Bacon's "New Atlantis." I am sure that it exists somewhere in all its perfection of Art and Nature. It may be an astral land – or a secret occult centre – or a retreat of Initiates of a spiritual Order. Or, more marvellous, extra-terrestrial visitants have it as a sane place where they can study and meditate in peace, away from earthly tumult.

AIDEN: You know too clearly what you want – so this blocks your actual adventure! You need the imagination of a child, not the schedule of an alumni! Try not to expect the unexpected. You find yourself before a doorway above which is a symbol of a rampant lion. Try and enter.

SOPHIA: This is quite easy. I go through. Then I hastily turn back. I face a real lion! Aiden, this is pretty obvious. He looks somewhat aggressive... did you create him? Or did Elaine? ... I am shocked. The lion is addressing me in my native tongue. I will translate into English. It's very clear...

LION: I am myself and need no Creator. Nor do you. You are arrogant, to hide your fear of being controlled. You would prefer me to be a lioness – say, Sekhmet!

SOPHIA: I feel annoyed. I say: "I never asked for you so what are you doing here interrupting my trance?" He answers: "Aiden is your earthly Path Guide. I am your Spirit Teacher. Do you accept me, or would you prefer some human Professor?" I say hastily that I do accept him. Otherwise I should have failed in my first test.

* * * Everything goes misty. I experience a change of state. It's hard to report in English but I'll try. You see I am in the dreamland of my childhood, where I used to find refuge from my father's lessons. I found it when I refused to blow up a useless "drop-out" instead of the Golden Gate Bridge. I had pictured the man as a Romany. My father on our Council had just evicted a Romany camp. They were obstructing the building of steel works necessary for our State. They had to move into our forest where I found them – in my dreams. I dreamt I was taught the Bohemian Tarot and how to create animated friends from my toys. I admit I did have a toy lion called Leo. I used to cry into his mane when I found my physics lesson too hard.

The lion is saying that he had come to me as Leo and took me on magical journeys to the gypsy camp. Now he would take me there again. I would meet their King!

I am entering deeper into trance. It is now as real as everyday life... I will try and describe this place – I love it! There is a magnificent log fire and I realise it is in our Bohemian Wood. Men and women are busy preparing for some celebration. The women are rolling out some peculiar looking grey flat bread, and the men are decanting what looks like some beer or wine. It is a funny colour – greeny-brown with a strong rather pleasant odour – I wonder what they make it of?

I love the music. It is stringed, with drum beats. Suddenly there is a hush. From a hidden grove a young man is led forward. Despite the cold weather – some snow is still lying on tree branches – he is only wearing a shirt and denims. There are questions and answers from Elders, both men and women, and he appears to have answered successfully. I realise he has passed varied trials for courage and loyalty. * * *

Now I am witnessing a ritual that would have fascinated Queen Marie of Rumania, my ancestor, who honoured Romanies, and wrote a book about them. This was the crowning of their King!

Now the scene is attaining a new depth. The company are not only with their ancestors, who show themselves, but with their descendants, now not born!

What I am witnessing is the ceremonial and spiritual crowning of a King who has been chosen by the ancestors and acclaimed by the people. I won't describe this . . . it is holy and private. I am in an altered state of consciousness. The lion is shining with golden light. We are surrounded by rainbow colours. My happiness is suddenly interrupted by the lion.

"Sophia," he says. "Have you any wish?" I was about to say that I wanted for nothing – I was in bliss – when suddenly the image of my father came before me. "I would like my father to be here," I said. Just for an instant I have a glimpse of my father's state – melancholia giving way to amazement as he tries to see despite such strong light. He reaches out his hands to the company . . . then I lose the connection. I am in darkness, floating . . . I have never known a trance like this.

AIDEN: That is because you are not in an unreal world but an alternative reality. Do you wish to return or stay?

SOPHIA: I love being here! But where am I? * * * I find myself of all places, in a deserted chapel! There is a stone altar and some broken statues of mediaeval saints. I like the weeds growing through the floor. Outside are the most remarkable gargoyles! Plainly they depict unpopular clerics amidst demons acting as water outlets. Then I observe a heap of black clothing in the porch. To my surprise the heap moves and a human being sits up! She is conventionally dressed and her voluminous black cloak has an Astrakhan collar. She speaks in my native tongue: "So you have come to join me in my protest?"

"I would," I reply, "if I knew what you were protesting about." She looks at me with bright grey eyes. "I am protesting against folly," she says. "I am surrounded by fools in the government, in the church, in my school. I am a headmistress by the way, so I can only get here at weekends and during the holidays. My Inspiration is Erasmus – You know his 'Praise of Folly' illustrated by Holbein?"

I look around. "But where are the others?" I ask. "The press – the police – other protesters?" "They are the fools against whom I protest," she says. "I am a heretic hermit. Admittedly I have to cook my husband's lunch shortly, and my children will be back from a nature walk – but I've been here for my usual night's vigil. I feel I am more sane in the peace of nature here. I've only got forty minutes for you to join me. It's cold but you may share my cloak."

This is the strangest meditation I have ever experienced! This is not for forty minutes. Suddenly I am in a changed state of consciousness. The heavens open to reveal innumerable stars. Above all there is the sound of celestial music that transports my soul. The Light of Vesta is revealed to me... I am in the Land of Macaria, and I sit within the cloak of its Queen. But even as I awaken spiritually, the lion draws me back.

"Sophia, have you any request?"

Once more I feel like replying that I am in a state of divine awakening, and need nothing. But suddenly, I think of the Lover with his terrible companions in the wretched basement. I say: "I would like the man I called the Lover to be here." From far away I see the form of the Lover looking young and cheerful as he used to be. I strain to hear his words. "I learn from you, Sophia Dorothea, I shall be a hermit."

I try to bring all this beauty with me as I return from my journey. Then I understand. The lion presents me with a Rose, with luminous petals that fly far and wide.

END OF TRANCE.

ALL GIVE THEIR REPORTS AND SEND OUT RAYS OF HARMONY. THANKS ARE GIVEN TO THE DEITIES. A FEAST IS ENJOYED IN A HUT IN THE WOOD WITH A CANDLE LIGHTED TO VESTA.

End of Rite.

Sources: "The New Atlantis," Francis Bacon. "A Description of the Famous Kingdom of Macaria." Samuel Hartlib, as presented to the Long Parliament during the English Commonwealth. (It was well received, but the ideal State has yet to materialise.) "The Chymical Wedding of Christian Rosenkreutz," Johann Valentin Andreae. "Viatorium," Michael Maier. "The Rosicrucian Enlightenment," Frances A. Yates, pub. by Ark. "The Tempest," Shakespeare. "The Magic Flute (Die Zauberflote): Libretto," Wolfgang Amadeus Mozart. "Rosa Alchemica," W.B. Yeats. "Isis in Bohemia," Annals of the USA political club, 20th Century. "The Emerald Tablet of Hermes Trismegistus" as found in a vault by Apollonius of Tyana.

"Maya and Her Firebird"

INTRODUCTION TO CHAPTER 6
"WE ARE ALL GODS. SO IS THE CAT."

I first became aware of apartheid, the exclusion of one lot of people from another, at my "posh" school in England. It was Anglican High Church. However, we had a sub-class of humans living in the same house who were called "Miners' Daughters." This was a charitable Christian work. Their community in Wales was poor – very, very poor. We were never allowed to speak to them, nor have any awareness of their names or who they were. They worked in secret. We were to leave our beds drawn back to air before the Miners' Daughters had to make them correctly. I used to listen to our fellow students talking about them. "They dress up on their days off just like us. What cheek."

I was aware that Roman Catholics, our "opposition", had the same attitude. I was talking to an Irish child abuse survivor, who said a nun had told her: "You come from nothing. You are nothing." Another victim told me she kept quiet for sixty years about her time enduring years of abuse. She never even told her husband. To be a victim was your fault – your inferiority. Then she decided to speak out. She testified in court. Her behaviour was not approved of by one old woman who told the press: "I never heard of these nasty things when I was a girl. I was brought up properly. No wonder their Reverences kept quiet about nastiness. It gives the church a bad name."

Through the Fellowship of Isis, I wished to bring the honour given to the few to all. I observed that men paid money but had no respect for pretty young girls stripping naked to music. Yet millions were deeply moved by a young woman being dressed. She was given crown, robe and sceptre to music. She was anointed with oil reserved only for her, holy oil for her status alone.

In our Ordination of a Priestess ceremony each woman is given a crown, a Priestly stole and a wand. She is anointed with holy oil. As for Priests, they are given a mitre, a robe and a staff. They too are anointed. We now have thousands of Queens and Popes. And each one is special.

In England I had been brought up to fight evil, taught by Victorian stories. My task as a Christian was to find evil and fight it. You just had to find the evil, defeated by heroes, Abraham Lincoln, Charles Dickens, Florence Nightingale, Lord Shaftesbury and William Wilberforce. I found Mahatma Ghandi. I became a Pacifist.

The concentration camps dampened my belief in peace process. Then I joined the positive thinkers, who came from America. They believed the way to help the world was to follow the three Wise Monkeys, who see no evil, hear no evil, speak no evil. This total denial of negativity, "the Dark", "the left-hand path" affirmed that we were to propagate the Light, and so receive health, popularity and abundance. I remember one lady saying: "I have no money. I got flu. I must be thinking wrong . . ."

You see the religion I was taught declared we were nothing, creatures created and therefore subject to the power of the Creator. I noticed most Gods of various faiths heartily despised and periodically destroyed their own creation – as true artists will ever do in quest of perfection.

In our faith I was taught that "humanity was born and conceived in sin, through the disobedience in daring to procreate." Like other religions, we had to appease the wrath by a time-honoured ritual of sacrifice. We could never be born like the Creator's Only Son – we were like androids; but the ancient cannibal ritual of eating perfect victims was sacramentally enacted. "Natives" ate a missionary, and so gained his boat and his magic. We did this to the Son, ritually eating Him. Our Priests, and only they, magically transformed bread and wine into the Son's body. We performed "consubstantiation" – God and the food. Roman Catholics did it properly through "transubstantiation." Only their Priests could do this. So the old woman who wished us to keep quiet to save their Reverences was logical. They had to keep the Priests performing the sacrifice or she would never attain heaven.

I examined what other faiths had to offer. Classical religion only offered you Divinity if an amorous God or Goddess raped you. In Babylon the dead had no hope. They crawled on their stomachs eating dust forever. Only Her Lover was saved by the Goddess Ishtar.

Still, you did have some sort of life in Hades, depressing though it was. Buddhism removed these fears of the soul's sufferings by saying we had none. There was no cruel God - or Gods - because there weren't any. I could, like Kwan Yin, gain enlightenment at the price of losing my individuality and, like Kwan Yin, becoming a man. Only men could get enlightened. Only in the Mystery Orders did spiritual truth emerge. We in the Fellowship of Isis open the Mysteries to all – and free!

Now I realise that we will never regain our divinity by playing mind systems. What is glorious now is that Awakening comes usually unexpectedly. This Divine Reality from which we have all been born transcends both time and space.

Many people tell of this onset of mystical consciousness. To me it came through total despair. If I had had a gleam of hope I would have gone off to lunch. But on the 30th October, 1945, I saw the earth as dominated by evil, a triangle like a pyramid, dominated by a cruel little boy astride the earth like a Colossus. I heard a voice saying to reverse the triangle. It became the Holy Grael. When I put the triangles together, they formed the Star of David. When the two points converge round the centre in a geometrical diamond, you have the mystical Diamond of Perfection, blending high and low.

My form of mystical consciousness of emblems comes through "omniscience", so I am a writer, playwright and painter. But others awaken to "omnipotence" – the use of energies. Many have the lovely unity with Nature through "omni-presence". And we are only at the portals of the Labyrinth that is complete. But we have to travel through time and place to Centre. And as we come nearer to the central Matrix, we have no enemies, and evil has been transmuted into its own good. Duality teaches Truth. Unity brings Love. Harmony prevails.

CHAPTER 6: YUCATAN

ALCHEMICAL RITE
PART ONE: THE NARRATION
"TO REACH THE HEIGHTS WE NEED TO PLUMB THE DEPTHS."

HOST IN YUCATAN IS LEON KINICH. VISITANTS: PATH GUIDE: ELAINE, PRIESTESS OF ALCHEMY. HELPER: AIDEN, PRIEST OF ALCHEMY. DEIRDRE OF THE VISIONS, ORACLE.

KINICH: I call upon the Fellowship of Isis from despair. Our once mighty civilisation stemming from the continent Atlas, surrounded by the Atlantic Ocean has now fallen under foreign rule. We are poor derided, downtrodden. We have betrayed our country by losing the power to resist. Weakened by dreams, we have forgotten our Goddess Maya in Her own land of the Mayans. I hear one of your visionaries has seen Maya, and that Her Golden Condor has come to you. I seek Her Oracle for guidance to restore our ancient faith.

ELAINE: We are honoured to fulfil your wish. Our Oracle, Deirdre of the Visions, has already received a vision in the Heavens of Maya. Our Priest of Alchemy, Aiden, will invoke the Goddess.

AIDEN: I invoke the aid of the Goddess Maya, through Her veiled Priestess. Holy Maya, You appear across the sky as a copper-coloured Sun. Your children are lost to Divinity. Help us to restore your faith in this your land.

ORACLE OF THE GODDESS MAYA

Do not despair! In My Thirteen Heavens, humans are courageously facing the passing of the fourth sphere of emotional control to the fifth sphere of the consciousness of passions. There are many races who attain initiation easily, as they have never endured the ordeal of physical incarnations, through the labyrinth of space and time. Those in solar bodies are glorious as Gods and Goddesses. But you, the suffering ones, only regain your true Being, Divinity, through ordeals. Trials seem cruel, but know that the Mothers and Fathers who have given you birth have put you to school in planetary evolution. And though you endure unspeakable pain, you win a wonder unknown even to Deities. You have found your true originality peculiar to each one of you! Without a single soul, the peacock-starry sky would be incomplete.

The Plumed Serpent of Divine Energy rises slowly within each of you, and when you win back your birthright, you have no spectacular fall! Those spirits who fly too high have to return to Mother Earth in shame. You deal with humiliation, guilt, evil passions daily, not as the leaping jaguar, but rather have a sure slow progress, like a quiet cat who has learnt to rest before a hearth fire!

AIDEN: We give thanks for the heartening Oracle of the Goddess Maya as She opens Her great dark eyes and smiles!

ELAINE: We request you to give us your narration of your soul's journey. Tell us why you feel desperate to save your land.

THE NARRATION

KINICH: My very name betrays my divided soul. I was born of a Spanish sailor and a Mayan woman Shaman. Both taught me their religion, and both had much in common. Our Mayans had, through Toltec and Aztec invasions, destroyed our country through human sacrifice. Our loving Kukulkan declared to His people: "Give me your hearts." Unfortunately, as is the way of organized religion, this request was misunderstood. I feel the grief of the God Kukulkan at this evil distortion of his loving words.

When I turned to my sailor father's religion, I believed at first that his church only had symbolic sacrifices, infinitely superior to the faith of my mother. However, I was disillusioned when I discovered that my father's ancestors had burnt tens of thousands of people to placate a God of Love. They made fools of heretics by putting pointed caps on their heads and garments painted with flames, to indicate that they would burn forever in "hell."

AIDEN: You dwell too much in the past. We are civilized now. There is progress through the rational sciences, and organized social welfare for all. Why not join our modern world of democracy, freedom and progress?

KINICH *(LAUGHS BITTERLY)*: How can I be enthusiastic about the British and Americans who dropped two atomic bombs? So much for science! Their technology will be the end of our planet through pollution. The money grabbers are cutting down our rain forests in stupid greed.

ELAINE: True. But individual people are far better off. They are healthier and live much longer.

KINICH: But at whose expense? Ours! To me the most detestable sight is to see poor Mexicans attending a clinic to sell a kidney for a rich European. All over the Middle East and India the poor show the scars on their bodies where they have donated vital organs to extend the life span of the rich. Destitute families sell their children to paedophiles in order to eat.

ELAINE: You have succeeded in filling me with horror. All my Liberal Optimism fades faced with evil. We in the "white" countries are as Vampires, feeding off the poor. You have all the skill in manipulating our emotions that will make you become President of your Republic!

KINICH: Gladly – if I have a solution. I have none. I have faith in no-one – except my dog. Here he is – he's called Hunhau.

ELAINE: All that you have described is a nightmare, a distorted holographic dream. Humans, not the Gods, distort divine teachings. We need to attain a Causal Realm of being. Are you willing to enter trance with myself as Shaman?

KINICH: I would not trust a man. He would try and get hold of my soul. But I trust a woman. I trust you . . .

HE LIES ON A COUCH WITH HIS EYES CLOSED. THERE IS SOFT MUSIC AND THE SCENT OF INCENSE. ELAINE PUTS FLOWERS BY HIM.

ELAINE: I can't get you into trance, because you are extremely suspicious! You have one eye open. You need extra Shamanic Help.

AIDEN PICKS UP A DRUM

AIDEN: Kinich, magical bird, come with your magical wings! We shall leave you for forty minutes.

THE COMPANY LEAVES KINICH BY HIMSELF, SAVE FOR HIS DOG, WHICH LIES AS GUARDIAN AT HIS FEET. FROM AN ADJOINING ROOM COMES THE SHAMANIC HEART-BEAT OF THE DRUM.

PART TWO: ALCHEMICAL RITE
THE OCEAN ISLAND OF MAYAPA.
"FIRE AND WATER ARE LOVERS."

IN THE HIDDEN TEMPLE OF THE MAYAS
TRANCE JOURNEY

SHAMAN, ELAINE. HELPER, AIDEN.

AIDEN: We are in this hidden Temple of the Mayas, concealed from curious eyes by high and ancient trees, and blessed by bird song. Birds are our only visitors. Kinich, I am here to help you if you lose your way.

ELAINE: Kinich, you do not speak . . . You are too deeply in trance. Speak to us as you make your way. Where are you?

KINICH: I am lost in gloomy darkness. I am descending into the depths. Yet my heart is filled with a nostalgic ecstasy. I know this way. This was made thousands of years ago. It is a journey through the earth, yet I am surrounded by hundreds of spectres who float above their skulls. These skulls gleam with supernatural green light.

ELAINE: Where are you going?

KINICH: I am drawn by a passionate longing to reach the Sacred Golden Temple of thirteen ascending octaves of Sacred Sound that is concealed, and yet sheds its holy light. The music is not heard by the profane but sends its Divine music throughout the starry heavens. Yet I am impeded by a feeling of guilt. My heart is poisoned with hatred at the evils that pollute our earth. I pray for help to the Winged Serpent Kukulkan to awaken!

AIDEN: There is someone coming behind you from the light. Look round! Here is your Guide.

KINICH: I look round. I am disgusted. I see what I most despise – an arrogant richly dressed tourist – a woman in sunglasses. She is impertinent enough to keep taking photographs!

I cannot see her clearly because she stands against the light. She says in an American accent: "My legs are killing me!" She produces a bottle of fizzy drink. "I'm parched. I'm going, I need water. I must sit down." She is looking around her. "Fabulous!" she says. "There's some sort of hidey hole! Let's go there!" In a dark wall I now see a door and through this is a cave. I follow the woman in. We both squat on the floor on a rug which she spreads out for us.

"You look pretty done in," she says. "It's a nice interesting resort, Latin America, with nice excursions. But I suppose you're just exhausted. And these natives do beg. I'm running out of change. I'm sorry for the poor but there's too many of them outside our hotel."

Suddenly total rage consumes me. I find myself declaring that I am a native Indian as she calls us – and a torrent of anger carries me away, overcoming all longing for spiritual peace. She is sitting with her arms round her knees, and as a final insult calmly finishes her mineral water, and sucks a peppermint.

I turn on her. "There you sit," I say, "well fed, with you white people living off our vital organs while you strip our country of our trees and dry up our rivers and threaten our earth with atomic war!"

The woman says: "And are you people so peaceful and good?" Now I feel ashamed. "No," I say. "We did great evils in the past that I can hardly bear to contemplate. So I see no hope for us humans. I only trust my dog."

The woman says: "There are always two ways of looking at things. You see a blood-stained body without a heart – I see a shining crystal skull attached to a God with a ruby heart. What are you looking at now?"

I look around me. I see an empty crumbling cell with human and animal bones. There is no water and I feel we are trapped.

"So we are," says the woman. "Not just metaphorically. Do you observe a landslide?"

To my terror I see our entrance is blocked by a fall of earth. I start clawing at the earth to escape. I command her to help, but she sits quietly for all the world like a complacent cat. She is combing her long black hair . . .

Now I have a new fear upon me – a fear of the supernatural . . . Yes, I like mythological beings that lived in past ages. But this is *now!* I am in the presence of a *witch*. I know they abound these days in the West as they are no longer burnt. I know now why people burnt and drowned witches. They were afraid of them. So am I. I see her shadow in the form of a huge dark cat silhouetted against the wall. It is hissing . . . !

"Aiden, help me. I am lost in some underground hell with a witch and a black cat. I never believed in them. Now I do. *Protect me!"*

AIDEN: Ask her name.

I look in the woman's eyes and I say: "Tell me your name."

Suddenly a miracle happens! I ascend in expanded consciousness throughout a mighty four level pyramid. The whole underground realm becomes the base of the pyramid. We, the woman and our dog and cat are standing in the centre surrounded by trees whose roots extend like a grid about us. The woman takes me by the hand and she opens her dark eyes and she laughs.

"Welcome home, Kukulkan," she says. We do not need to rise for we extend through the pyramid, and our heads reach the stars and are crowned with rays of Light. Round our bodies are flowers and fruits, all the bounty of the earth bestowed throughout the ages. I see the past and I see the future and all is well. But she has still not told me her name.

She says: "Kinich, what will you do to create a world that mirrors forth its Divine Origin?"

I remember long ago some woman said I would help the people by rulership. I say: "I would bring humans, animals, plants, the sacred gifts offered by Nature Spirits. We will force none, however helpless, but bring honour to all even through loving one creature. All are born of the Mothers. Heaven and earth are one through harmony. My despair is transformed to Bliss."

The woman ascends into the sky and her body is shining with copper-coloured Light. Her hair is raven and flows down her back and she is seated cross-legged from East to West across the sky. There is the singing of a woman's voice ascending in octaves through the four worlds.

"Know me as She Who holds Past, Present and Future as One. Hear my Name. I am Maya."

Even as she says the word, I see the sky filled with the mighty golden wings of a Golden Condor, with a small blue bird above him. As the Divine Goddess disperses Her light through the cosmos, I hear Her words.

"Kinich, You are the Avatar of my Consort, the God Kukulkan. You have returned upon the earth with your blue Firebird, Kinich, to bring fire to the fearful, gentleness to fiery warriors, and Love and Wisdom to all. As you enter the haven of sleep you shall awaken to my Paradise of Mayapan, ocean island surrounded by the ocean of air and water. When you awaken as the sun rises I will bring to your mind what you will act during each day. You will bring my blessings wherever you prevail. Return to earth and bring this enlightenment to your friends who have come far to be with you."

I am slowly returning from ecstasy and feel now a peaceful Love. I know now that each man and woman and creature must find their own way through the jungle by the mighty river to reach their own way to Heaven, as a river finds its way to the starry sea.

END OF TRANCE.

KINICH SLOWLY RECOVERS FROM TRANCE BUT KEEPS A STATE OF BLISS. THEY ALL GIVE THANKS TO THE DEATHLESS DEITIES AND OFFER THEIR CREATIVE INTENTIONS TO BRING THE EARTH TO PERFECTION. THEY SHARE A FEAST OF FRUIT AND WINE WITH THE INHABITANTS OF A NEARBY VILLAGE, THE WOMEN IN THEIR BEAUTIFUL WHITE EMBROIDERED DRESSES. AMONG THEM ARE TOURISTS, WHO DISGUISE THEIR STATUS AS PILGRIMS BY WEARING DARK GLASSES.

End of Rite.

Sources: "Mexico and Central American Mythology," Irene Nicholson, Panther. "North American Indian Mythology," Cottie Burland. "Atlantis and the Giants," Denis Saurat. "Queen of the Sun," Emory J. Michael, Prescott. AZ. "The Tenth Insight: Holding the Vision, (Celestine Prophecy)," James Redfield. "Maya, Goddess Rites for Solo Use," Olivia Robertson. "Short Stories," Jorge Luis Borges. "The Old Man and the Sea," Ernest Hemingway.

"The Charm of Wings"

INTRODUCTION TO CHAPTER 7
"LIVING IN A VIRTUAL WORLD."
"TO LIVE IN HEAVEN IS TO LIVE NOW."

Like many Bohemians, I have been rebuked for taking things lightly: "To laugh wildly in the face of death." (Shakespeare) So we should do, if we recognise Death as the sham it is.

To give an example: "The Chymical Wedding of Christian Rosenkreutz" has been described as a hoax, perpetrated by its brilliant author, Valentin Andreae. One of the "absurd" scenes is when Cupid pricks the hand of Rosenkreutz with a dart which draws blood. Cupid is not acceptable as a real being but as an allegory with his darts.

Not at all. In that strange world of psychic Rescue Work which I sometimes help out, I lost my temper, furious at the games played by evil doers. I did notice that they were trying so hard to be bad, but were amateurs compared with some members of religious establishments. Anyway the whole occult matter was brought to a happy conclusion by the sudden apparition I saw of a tiny naked boy made of golden metallic light. His hair and wings were opaque, of a vermilion-red. The hair was strange – like wool. His features looked Indian.

I loved his glorious smile showing shining white teeth. He lifted my arms above my head and peered down at my face three times from above. Then he vanished and all evil was dispelled by love and laughter. I found he had left a memento – two blood-red thorn marks on the palm of my right hand.

Humanity is now venturing upon the no-man's land of the cyber world. Nothing is what it seems. A hopeful schoolgirl dreams of a perfect lover and finds him on her computer as a noble image. But if she is unwary enough to meet him – he is old and terrifying. A young man is tempted to take a job in a foreign country – and arrives there having sold all his savings. He is trapped into a crime ring, and dares not escape because he is an illegal immigrant.

How can we protect our children and ourselves from a holographic world? We have a choice. We can retreat from the virtual world, and ban all computers and cell phones and "twitters" and "facebooks" and settle in an ideal retreat centre. Or is it?

We face the same problems with people who can present themselves as spiritually fascinating and exciting as any "wolves" in the cyber world. I see the Vulnerable as a character in Beatrix Potter's heroine in her children's book "Jemima Puddleduck." Jemima was a duck and was safe with fellow ducks who all chanted "Pitpuck puddle-duck." But she strayed. Jemima met a gentleman in a smart waistcoat. He with beautiful red fur ears and a long bushy red tail. Jemima got herself a blue bonnet and met him secretly in a wood. He told her to bring him presents including sage and onions . . . This tale ended correctly because the farm sheepdog ate the gentleman with red whiskers, rescuing Jemima from her destined end on the farmer's dinner table.

That was the way it was. We vulnerable dreamers were under the protection of male members of one's family and tribe if we obeyed the rules. There was the sheriff, and the police, and they were backed by the military. Faced now with planetary danger, women, the lost half of humanity, wonder what they can do to save our earth, our home.

I have a curious answer in an incident that occurred in the Dublin Theosophical Society. It was in the "fifties." I was arguing with a woman who said that the Roman Catholic Church had taken the left hand path. At that time I was practising seeing only the Good In All, and disapproved of people with conspiracy theories. These targeted the Vatican, the Freemasons, the Elders of Zion, the Illuminati, and, of course, Witches.

However, something odd happened. The woman later said she had been standing by me as I happily conversed with a Spiritual Healer. She claimed she got struck on her side by an electric shock. When she got home she took out her latchkey. It was twisted beyond use! She had to have her door broken into. She wouldn't allow the matter to rest. A locksmith told her it was impossible to twist steel except professionally. She contacted me. I could offer no explanation – but felt rather pleased somehow . . . The Healer also declined responsibility. We felt the incident reflected on our positive reputation. The lady then drew it to the attention of Theosophy Headquarters in London. They had no explanation.

I assumed that Deity was showing me that I was right and that the lady was wrong. How reassuring . . . But now I have another explanation. Recently in a group, a woman felt she was being pushed too far, and could not write her book, I gave her a psychic reading, and as she left she said: "Thank you. You have given me my key. Now I feel free to write my book." I noticed that she was free of her group – and of myself. She had found her own key.

So now I understand that one person's key will not work for another. No one holds the Keys of Heaven and Hell, nor can they save or damn anyone. There is only one key to heaven and hell. It depends on yourself and in which direction you face.

CHAPTER 7: EIRE

ALCHEMICAL RITE
PART ONE: THE NARRATION
"MAGIC FINDS YOU UNEXPECTEDLY."

HOSTESS IN EIRE IS KAREN ETAIN. SCENE IS IN A FLAT IN A HOUSING ESTATE OUTSIDE DUBLIN. VISITANTS: PATH GUIDE: AIDEN, PRIEST OF ALCHEMY. HELPER: ELAINE, PRIESTESS OF ALCHEMY. DEIRDRE OF THE VISIONS, ORACLE.

KAREN: I call upon you, as like so many of my generation in this country I have reached the crossroads. I am caught by a longing for the unseen world of Faery, and my unbelief in all superstitions, whether religious or occult. Help me to find my way. We are of Eire, Land of Destiny – Inis Faile. We have lost our ancient past, and are shipwrecked in the present; with no more faith we have no future.

ELAINE: You are not alone in this mad world! Many people seeing the earth crumbling under them; doubt the reality of any heaven. Some young people in many countries are taking their own lives – even school-children. Parents move heaven and earth to protect them from abuse, yet do not believe in heaven or hell. Only the Goddess can help us, if we believe She exists! In this extremity let us invoke the Oracle. To us who love Her, She holds the Stone of Destiny.

AIDEN *(LIFTS UP HIS DRUIDIC STAFF)***:** I invoke the Great Queen of Eire, The Morrigan, who with Her Divine Consort the Dagda Mor presides over Time.

DEIRDRE IS IN TRANCE AND SPEAKS:

ORACLE OF THE MORRIGAN

You who call upon me are for the most part prisoners in passing time. I watch you with the love of a mother as you start your lives with the sacred Light shining within you. This may be seen by visionaries as a flame over a child's head. A baby is still in touch with the Eternal Land from which all come. Time is a beautiful pattern of rivers reaching the boundless ocean of space with its myriads of stars. But as a child grows older, those around it try to bring it to their own limited way of being, which is a timeline between life and death. So the child, in order to conform and please others, loses essential being, a link with the world beyond.

Radiation from brighter realms can bring fear and hostility from those who have lost this golden key. This was the way of Neanderthal man and many other primitive races. They still exist and have their honoured place as do all, as children of the Mothers, species who have the courage to have physical experiences.

For Homo Sapiens, the time is now when a new race is coming into being. This new humanity will be more heart-centred and have spiritual vision. It is for women to calm men's fear, for women usually long for this coming. No people can endure alien or foreign occupation, however well-meaning! But children are accepted. No man can resist the smile of his own baby!

ELAINE: We give thanks for this inspiring Oracle. Karen, does this help you? Tell us what you feel.

THE NARRATION

KAREN: It doesn't help me one bit. Alternative book shops are full of this sort of stuff. And I adore it but don't believe a word. I suppose it's part of my background. My father is a Protestant and a very clever surgeon. My mother is a very efficient nurse – they met in a hospital in Dublin, and she is also a very strict Catholic. I was baptised a Catholic. But my father said it was brain-washing! My mother had a Lourdes grotto in the garden, while my father had a large photograph of Charles Darwin in his study. The only sacraments they shared were Easter Day dinner with chocolate eggs for my sake, and a Christmas Dinner with turkey. I was an only child so they both wanted me to take after them. My father thought "Karen" as my first name was sufficiently secular – my mother liked the Romantic "Etain'" from "The Immortal Hour", though she wished there was a Saint Etain. That I might fulfil the role was her secret dream.

No-one can say I didn't try to please. At first I liked the way of my mother. I read an anthology of Yeats' poetry. I avidly read about the doings of Women of the Golden Dawn, and for a while in my early teens grew my hair long, and assumed a languorous dreamy expression – though really I was as psychic as an old boot! I did various courses on spiritual development from Arizona – nothing happened. It got rather expensive.

The crisis came when I had to have an operation to remove a melanoma, because I had been lying for hours in the sun, pretending I was in California, and one of my courses recommended the life-giving rays of the sun that healed all ills. Luckily I had avoided hallucinogenic substances of Akhenaton's Sun, the Aten. I have a Celtic skin and just got freckles.

So I decided to follow the Path of Practical Science. I took my father's advice and studied medicine. With his help I am now a qualified, first year Doctor. At first it was wonderful. I was Daddy's girl. He preferred my company to that of my mother's. He brought me all round Dublin, introducing me as "My only daughter – a medical student." I got a whole new lot of boyfriends. Before I had been taken out by idealists, pacifists like myself, and avid fans of various groups. But I never got deeply involved because I was not attracted by the physical world – in any aspect. Anyway, drugs just made me sick and I prefer classical music.

Both worlds offered to me by my parents were lacking in substance. We had no apparitions of the Blessed Virgin in housing estates; there was not a miracle in sight. My mother was not happy. She did her duty and obeyed the rules, her marriage and our home were extremely clean and proper, but there was no joy nor laughter. My father would hide in his study, reading abstruse scientific works. And neither could fight the most terrible enemy of all: death.

They tried. But I saw through my mother's faith in the next world, because of her excessive fear of illness and horror when her friends died. My father had no belief in an afterlife. Or so he said. But I felt his insistence on the unreality of a soul separate from a body came from some sort of hidden fear, kept at bay by denial.

They say I have a good career ahead of me. The future of Ireland, once land of saints and scholars, is now to cater for useful doctors and nurses. But I feel I did have a soul once, but now it is starved. Can your Fellowship, your imaginary Goddesses help me? Have I a soul?

DEIRDRE: I am receiving a message from the Morrigan Herself: "We can only help you if you help yourself."

PART TWO: ALCHEMICAL RITE
TIR NA NOG, LAND OF YOUTH.
"ECSTASY COMES WITH SURRENDER OF FALSE SELF."

IN THE HIDDEN SHRINE OF THE TUATHA DE DANANN

ELAINE: In this apartment in the Land of Destiny let us create a hidden shrine of the Tuatha De Danann who dwell in eternal realms, invisible to our mortal eyes.

SACRED PAINTED TAPESTRIES ARE PLACED IN THE FOUR QUARTERS, AND INCENSE AND CANDLES ARE LIGHTED. ALL ARE ANOINTED BY ELAINE ON THE BROW WITH WATER FROM THE SACRED WELL OF THE GODDESS BRIGID. DANA AND THE MORRIGAN ARE ALSO INVOKED, WITH THEIR SACRED GODS, MANANNAN MAC LIR, LUGH OF THE LONG WHITE ARM OF LIGHT AND THE DAGDA MOR, DIVINE KING OF EIRE.

KAREN IS TOLD TO LIE ON A COUCH BEFORE THE ALTAR, EYES CLOSED THAT SHE MAY SEE BETTER. UNDER THE DIRECTION OF DEIRDRE, SHE ENTERS LIGHT TRANCE, WHICH DEEPENS AS THE SESSION PROCEEDS. CELTIC HARP MUSIC IS PLAYED BY ELAINE.

TRANCE JOURNEY

AIDEN: Karen Etain, you are now in the twilight zone between sleeping and waking. Only what you yourself hold to be true and good will be accepted by your soul. You feel the golden flow of Danann light through every part of your body.

AIDEN PASSES HIS HANDS OVER KAREN'S BODY, UNTIL THE ALCHEMISTS SEE A GOLDEN HAZE. DEIRDRE OBSERVES THAT KAREN'S SOUL IS A FEW INCHES ABOVE HER BODY. SHE IS TOLD TO RETURN TO HER BODY, SO THAT SHE MAY SPEAK, IN HALF-TRANCE.

AIDEN: Karen Etain, where do you find yourself?

KAREN: I find I am lying on the cold granite capstone of a great dolmen. It gives cold power through my body. It is increasingly cold and I find I am sinking into darkness. It is not a friendly darkness. It is as unfeeling as stone. I hear a woman's voice: "Karen Etain, I am your true mother. I have lent you for a while to mortals, that you may bring many to know their own lost Divinity. You will not bring pleasing astral visions which have been the joy and sorrow of this land. You will bestow the Shield of Brigid, which reflects the Truth and Her spear, which brings Justice and Compassion. In your land there are many who half dwell in our lovely Land of Tir Na nOg, Land of Youth, and gain little from their earthly experience. You will bring the spiritual sphere, which unites mind and heart, dreams and activity. But to do this you must choose to do this! For too long have you crushed your true self in the delusion that your being is true to yourself. You live a lie."

I find myself saying: "What lie?"

She replies, and I know Her for the Morrigan: "You pretend that your aim in life is honesty. It is not. You are starved for love which you are ashamed to acknowledge."

I answer: "Great Goddess, I feel the power of your mind that far exceeds any human mind that I have encountered. How can I find this aim, which is so deeply hidden that I cannot recognise it?" She replies: "Bright girl who loves clarity, you need to go to the Well at the World's End, and within you will find your answer."

"Ah," I reply. I need to drink from its waters. "Not exactly," replies the Goddess, and her voice becomes fainter. There is a whirling like countless snowflakes and I am caught in a gust of wind. I am rising from the dolmen and enter the rainbow beauty of a lovely landscape fairer than anything I have ever seen on earth. The colours from octaves of ascent intermingle with each other in ever-changing rainbows. The trees are singing with joy as they bear fruit and flowers at the same time, as here Time is everywhere, in a Celtic design on the woven cloth of space. The music comes from the colours and the colours from the music. Here are birds that are unafraid and perch upon my fingers and I feel the soft skin of a wolf who leans against me, to look with golden eyes into my own. There are people here, but no humans. They are either what some call extremely ugly or delightfully beautiful. They read my thoughts and I read theirs. And all say: "She is for the Well."

Suddenly I am there, at the Well at the centre of the world, a hub around which all rotates. I find long grasses at the edge of the Well twine around my ankles – suddenly they trip me up and I fall into black depths . . .

I find I am falling through the centuries. I have glimpses of humans, and the human lives are as transient flitting shadows – here and then gone – but their buildings remain far longer, and some are noble and others pretentious. And I can choose to project into any scene I choose. But I remember my aim, to find my destiny.

I land with a vulgar human bump. I am at the bottom of the Well, which is muddy with sharp stones. I hear a hearty laugh! And then I see my first Faery! I am surprised that he is so tall. He answers my thoughts.

"Surely you remember? We ascend through the four elements. You chose air and fire and water – I have earth and water and fire – once we have our fifth element, ether, we are on a similar level as humans – but with more Spirit as we seldom descend into matter, except for earth Initiation, as you are doing now. It's rough, isn't it Etain? Ready to come home?"

I have fallen down a well. And now I have fallen in love. He is the most gorgeous being I have ever seen. His long hair is like a raven's wing. His eyes are deep and penetrating. But what makes him Divine is his body. It is not composed of organic matter, but created of some form of metallic, bronze coloured energy. Every muscle shows. Also, what completes his splendour for me, he has long iridescent wings that reach from his head to his feet, as colourful as medieval stained glass. So that is where artists get their inspiration from! In the dark ages they could see into another world.

He answers my thoughts. "True. But the present race of man cannot develop without mind. You tread on one foot, feelings, and the other, cleverness. But to fly you need wings – two of them for balance."

"I feel that I have been summoned here for some purpose," I say.

"True. Not one of us can incarnate upon earth without a task. One is to give, the other to receive. You told your earthly friends you are at the crossroads. You need to make a choice. Will you stay here with me, Midir, leaving your earthly body, or will you return to earth and be a Doctor? There is a Doctor who would marry you if you are not adverse to the idea."

I say: "A medical partnership? I feel I would not be happy here with you if I neglected my work. The colours would lose their lustre and the music cease. So with heavy heart I say farewell to you for this earthly life-time."

As I begin to move away from the lovely Land of Youth, I hear the voice of Midir: "Don't be so sure of your farewell. We always have some of our children on earth . . ."

END OF TRANCE.

KAREN VERY SLOWLY RETURNS FROM TRANCE, SLIGHTLY SMILING. SHE JUST SAYS "THANK YOU" TO THE ALCHEMISTS, AND LETS DOWN HER HAIR, WHICH FALLS ABOUT HER SHOULDERS IN TWO RAVEN CASCADES. ALL GIVE THANKS ON THE BANKS OF A STREAM AND HAVE A FEAST. THEY SAY IN MAKING THEIR REPORTS THAT THEY HAVE FELT A WONDERFUL FLOW OF RAINBOW LIGHT AND HEARD THE SOUND OF A DISTANT IRISH HARP.

End of Rite.

Sources: "Verse Plays," W.B. Yeats, Clarendon Press, Oxford. "The Crock of Gold," and "The Demi-gods," James Stephens. "Songs from Leinster," Winifred Letts, "The Real Charlotte," Somerville and Ross. "Finnegan's Wake," James Joyce. "The Candle of Vision." AE (George Russell), Macmillan, London. "The Immortal Hour: A Drama," "The Divine Adventure" " Ioana," "Studies in Spiritual History," Fiona MacLeod. "Myths and Legends of the Celtic Race," T.W. Rollestone. "A Celtic Miscellany: Translations from the Celtic Literatures," Hurlston Jackson. "Celtic Wonder Tales," illustrated by Maud Gonne. Ella Young.

"The Disc Player"

INTRODUCTION TO CHAPTER 8

"TO EVOLVE THROUGH WIDER CONSCIOUSNESS IS TO HAVE GREATER POWER TO BE GOOD OR EVIL."

When I was young I was taught by Spiritual Guides about the evolution of the cosmos. They used a Woolworth's corkscrew with a green handle. I enjoyed my lessons, because I was never commanded to believe anything until I in my own truth agreed with it. This was unlike any other teaching that I had been subject to.

We began with a circle, a bottle ring that contained all that is. This was our corkscrew pushed together, so that the curves became one. It was in blackness. The dark was all right, part of it all. Then after a period of no-time the circle began to rotate. As it rotated it began to spread out into spirals – a screw. The screw began to subdivide into pieces, into every sort of being and thing. I could think of it going from right to left, as we open a bottle. Finally everything became scattered all over everywhere, loosely in twos.

Then came a happening, quite recently, on October 5th, 2012. It was like a spirit of fire going opposite to everything. This spirit began to make another corkscrew. It went in the opposite direction, left to right, through our one! Everything began to get together! The twos became one, and all existences joined the new corkscrew. Finally they became two circles again – the mouth of an invisible bottle! The circle stopped rotating and there was a silence. This went on until it vanished into darkness. After ages a new circle formed, and the same process started again. But each time it was different.

"What then was forever," I asked, "with spirals changing?" "Consciousness was forever," I was told. It was God. God (God-Goddess) was all that is. What was changing all the time was consciousness. Cosmic consciousness was our end and our beginning. We all came from the One. So I should give every person and creature and plant - Honour.

All my life I have had psychic visions, but the ones that I most value teach me something that I need to think about. So I shall share a recent experience, and my reader might help.

Last year, in Chicago at the Alexandria Lyceum of FOI on October 30th, 2011, I had a beautiful vision at dawn. From a room behind her there entered a young girl of holiness and innocence. She had amber-coloured hair and she wore a silver-white gown. I was later given an earthly name from the past, but I shall use "Sophia." The Divine Wisdom in feminine form.

This year, 2012, I received another visitation from this spiritual being, this time presenting a mystery. Here it is . . . She was on this occasion full of life and energy, as light as a fairy. Her clothes flowed about her as she played with discs, some very large, some small. They were all around her. I wondered what they were – too flat to hold liquid or fruit. Also they were spinning at various rates into spirals.

The vision faded, but the puzzle remained, and still does. I related these discs to crop circles which I have visited every year in Wiltshire. I consulted an occult in Glastonbury who told me she had seen fine golden discs when she was nine years old and these contained teachings.

I imagined primitive islanders before the coming of Westerners finding a ship-wrecked traveller who might have rescued his wind-up gramophone and some records. When saved by a passing ship he would leave the islanders a record but kept the gramophone.

The priests and wise women on the island would try everything to hear the heavenly singing and orchestra again from the record, but get no results. The gramophone record would be reverently honoured on their altar, hopefully presented with worship and prayers.

Are we like those islanders with all our evolving science? We are very clever, but we are like a deaf race left with the score of Beethoven's 9th Symphony. They could draw equations, numerical and calculus, and create theories from the score – but would never hear the music.

Such a disc could be held over the heart . . . Or used to open doors by pressing a right place . . . But I believe that only by inspired consciousness shall we find the Unveiled Isis. But where is our disc? When Isis is unveiled, both space and time change into a wider sphere – a greater spiral. We are living in one room in a mighty Temple, surrounded by beautiful mountains, rivers and trees. And friends we have long forgotten. Each of us has Awakening at a different time and place – and yet in all time we are there already.

The nice thing about mystical experience is that it is always unexpected. That is the Divine Surprise.

CHAPTER 8: THE AZORES

ALCHEMICAL RITE
PART ONE: THE NARRATION
"TO LIVE WITHOUT VISION IS TO BE BLIND TO ONE'S SOUL."

HOST IN THE AZORES IS OISIN MANUELE. SCENE: HIS GARDEN BY THE SEA. VISITANTS: PATH GUIDE: ELAINE. HELPER: AIDEN. ORACLE: DEIRDRE OF THE VISIONS. ALL ARE OF THE PRIESTHOOD OF ALCHEMY.

AIDEN: It is very kind of you to invite us to this lovely castle by the sea with its private beach. You have everything here to awaken your psychic faculties. One could see anything here! Why do you require the urgent assistance of the Fellowship of Isis?

OISIN: Because you stand for everything that my family fears.

ELAINE It sounds intriguing. Please be more specific. Let us have your narration.

OISIN: You will be moved by its tragic note, accompanied by the moaning of the sea. My father was an Irish aristocrat, who bought this castle as a basis for his life's work, discovering the lost island of Atlantis. He married a peasant girl in our local fishing village, and this was his and my undoing. For he aspired to the stars: she wished to be a successful business executive. She had thought of emigrating to the States, but my father turned up in the nick of time. At first they got on reasonably well. I was born, but what seemed a blessing – proved a bitter source of contention. He insisted on calling me "Oisin", the Irish hero who was enticed to the Many-Coloured land across the ocean by a faery. My mother added "Manuele" after a local millionaire, who became my Godfather. My father dreamed that I could revive the Irish branch of the Order of the Golden Dawn, and become a poet like Yeats, an artist like AE, the Bard of Eire. My mother planned on creating a fishing subsidiary, part of an American company that specialised in tinned factory salmon. Horrible, imprisoning fish and destroying their ancient life cycle culminating in this ocean.

Finally tragedy struck. My father was drowned during an exploration of a stone wall under the sea that he hoped was a part of the lost city of Poseidonis. My mother found he had lost his whole fortune with his expeditions and the publication of a splendid book with coloured illustrations, "The Lost Atlantis Revived." But instead of Atlantis rising from the sea, my father's coffin is lying beneath the ocean, martyr to The Cause. I can show you a photograph of The Submerged Wall that he used in his book. I added a tribute to my father in a new edition which I have produced on the Internet.

ELAINE: You seem all set to follow in your father's footsteps. How can we help?

OISIN: By awakening my psychic vision. Surely I should have clairaudience and clairvision like my father. They say that the Irish have these gifts. But I have tried every means – to no avail. I have sat in dark rooms trying to see the aura around everything. Not a glimpse. I have sat in the lotus position gazing into the depths. I cannot see even one nymph – the Goddess Cleito's Atlantean offspring. Salamanders elude me in the flames of my beach fire. I am forced to earn my living in the Civil Service in a job my Godfather got for me – nepotism! But I need to live in order to fulfil my dream. I want, like AE, to see the Gods and Goddesses. I wish to live in the world beyond ours in the eternal Land of Everlasting Youth.

ELAINE: You put the blame on your mother and on your Godfather. But you yourself block your soul, gifts inherited from your father. You yourself are your own gaoler in a material cell.

OISIN: What am I to do? How do I block my visions?

ELAINE: You do not in the first place block your soul. It is done for you at the very moment of birth.

AIDEN: Who can blame parents training their children to fit in with religions, historical and national custom? Very small babies are put under perpetual, loving pressure to be "normal." Apart from the obvious potty training, every move a baby makes is conditioned. They even now extend this to "mentally challenged" babies who may be aborted before they are born. The mothers make sure their babies have the right physique – and are taught acceptable behaviour. A mother used to submit to ministry of the clergy – but this has given way to the autocracy of the doctor. A problem is that what is regarded as abnormal and to be rejected – changes. So the child with spiritual genius is regarded as unbalanced, and to be rendered harmless, sedated with a drug now given to about 70 million children that can even cause death. At least baptismal water was physically harmless!

The most powerful weapon used by well-wishers on the rising generation is within everyone – a desire to please OTHERS. If this fails, violence follows. And the present norm is to be clever, practical, and not to "hallucinate". Any form of psychism is treated as an abnormality.

OISIN: I am beginning to see. We Bohemians pretend that we don't care what people think. We do. All our so-called eccentricity is aimed at impressing the public – we need a public to impress! What must I do to unblock?

AIDEN: You need continual moral courage. The essence of Alchemy is to find the hidden gold within yourself. Then what you experience will bring wider vision, which is the birthright of us all. You will no longer try to impress others. You will even endure being laughed at!

OISIN: Somehow I feel hopeful. I feel a tingling all over my body. I can see a pale light round Deirdre! She seems to be asleep.

DEIRDRE: I feel the Presence of Cleito of Atlantis. We can bring Oisin through the mystic doorway, where he may find the Golden Apples of the Sun, fruit of Atlantis.

ELAINE: Deirdre, I see you are entering trance. Oisin, we may start you on your journey to your lost Atlantis straight away, here by the sea. I shall be your Path Guide. All you need to do is to lie on the strand, and listen to the sea birds as they fly over the ocean towards the horizon.

PART TWO: ALCHEMICAL RITE
THE RISEN ATLANTIS.
"TO DREAM TRULY IS TO CREATE."

BY THE ATLANTIC OCEAN
TRANCE JOURNEY

PATH GUIDE: ELAINE. HELPER: AIDEN. ORACLE: DEIRDRE OF THE VISIONS.

AIDEN: Friends, already the Goddess has heard the prayer of Oisin that he may find his Land of Heart's Desire, the lost Atlantis.

ORACLE OF THE GODDESS CLEITO

I come to you in heavenly dreams when your souls like lovely seabirds arise from your nests, your material bodies. There is no human, however physically obsessed, who has no hidden dream of some lovely realm from which they have come. The planetary school you call earth has in reality many levels, and consciously humans dwell in only one sphere of the third dimension. They are blind and deaf to other levels above and below them. And this is necessary as incarnation is the human path of individual development. Each soul finds the pain and ecstasy of rebirth to another and wider sphere.

The time and space of every awakening is individual. All through human history have found Divine Being.

Now at the end of an Aeon when human spiritual evolution has the opportunity of general awakening, it is necessary for each man and woman to seize this chance because the Gates close as the New Aeon dawns. A new humanity is manifesting, and there is chance for each soul to awaken, however alarming this may be. The past must be respected. In reality, time is ever present in the Now. It is we who travel, not the eternal tapestry of The Fates.

AIDEN: Thanks are given to the Goddess Cleito.

ELAINE: Oisin, I see you are already in trance. We await your account. Do not lose the connecting link of my voice. Where are you?

OISIN: Funny you should ask that, because I don't know! I feel I have been asleep for a long time. I'm back at the place where my father was drowned by the Atlantean Wall – but he's here. He looks much the same, only younger, before his beard. He has been expecting me and shook me by the hand. It's real. I feel his warm grasp. He doesn't speak. What he wants me to do is to look to the West, out to sea. I want to talk to him – but he continues to point over the sea to the horizon.

At first I see nothing but a pale blue sky and white-crested waves. Then just above the horizon I see a golden disc. Some sort of UFO I expect. It is growing, larger and nearer . . . I overcome a feeling of fear because my father is no longer with me. The disc has grown many times larger than the sun. It rotates and from it come two dazzling white streamers like wings. I remember seeing pictures of the golden winged disc of Ancient Egypt – but never thought they were real. I try to stand firm, though my knees feel weak. I remember reading of some huge Falcon, Horus, and expect to see Him emerging from the disc.

What a relief. No terrible Falcon or Aztec War God rushes at me with bared teeth. Instead there appears a laughing girl who holds a green branch like a quince with small yellow fruit. She daintily steps forth from the Disc, which proceeds to leave her on the strand. It diminishes in rotation through great sweeping arcs across the sea. This, I thought, is the Sea God Manannan's Wheel. I never knew it really existed.

The girl can read thoughts. She says "Yes, Oisin. All sea spirits use these wheels."

"Then this is subjective?" I say. "Not at all," she answers, and suddenly I feel she is wise for her years. "What you dream of brings you to your own paradise. Every night use true vision and you go where you will. Dreams exist, but have not the same properties as those which are true and beautiful. There is only one standard to test a creation. Only Goodness is forever."

"Are you a Goddess?" I ask. "Do you ever incarnate on a material planet?"

"Let us sit in the sand," she says. "I will tell you how I did incarnate on your earth, but it is not an experience I would want to have again!"

"You mean you are too perfect?" I ask.

"In no way. I'm too much of a coward to face the earth again."

I feel offended. I say "Human life is not that horrible surely. Why did you come in the first place if you're so advanced?"

She sighs. "I see you're getting huffy. I'd better tell you why I came and why I left earth."

Now she shows me a series of images like a DVD. They are extremely beautiful, and from some higher realm. I see a golden orb like the sun, and within it is some extra-terrestrial Priest. The young girl is receiving instructions. Both the Priest and the girl are in bodies of pure light. She wants to give some message to earth people in her light body, but she is told this would not do. Human-beings would not endure nudity, and the Light would hurt them. They were arbiters of what she should wear – appropriate robes. They contributed to anything given to them, and were of course treated with respect.

I can see into the girl's mind. She doesn't like the robes. The only people she can use telepathy with are children. What is strange is that she never leaves the orb. The people are far below, tiny figures. But she can project to them and give them the message, which she does not properly understand. But as she projects, she begins to see below the earth's surface into horrific images of underground prisons. She was told that people were entrapped because they chose to do so – due to some illness called "obsession." The girl decides to project into such places to help, though she is warned against doing so. Now she makes a wonderful discovery! She has a twin brother on earth who has incarnated before. He stays, but finally she has had enough! Her brother is an extremist. She makes up her mind in future to avoid the physical world, which has no attraction for her, but to work occasionally in the dream world. There helpers travel at night. She finds they bring people lovely dreams. They dwell in heaven and visit earth when called upon, but always remain spiritually awake. Her brother does it the hard way and returns only when he has to.

I find I can't help laughing. Yes, men are like dogs. Women are like cats, and look after themselves. Then I have a shattering thought. She refers to a well-meaning twin brother who suffers on earth helping others. Surely this is not myself?

"Oisin," the girl says, "You need to travel. I have brought you to your Land of Heart's Desire to give you hope and strength for your work on earth which you do for love. You needed to find your way here because you have found you need your soul. Any time on earth when your work is too cruel, you may now travel here, and see things in proportion. Earth and heaven are one when joined by a Rainbow of Joy and Beauty."

END OF TRANCE.

OISIN COMES BACK FROM TRANCE VERY SLOWLY. HE SAYS THAT IT IS TRUE THAT HIS WORK IN THE CIVIL SERVICE IS TO DEAL WITH THE PROBATION SERVICES FOR PRISONERS. THEIR LIVES ARE OFTEN HARROWING. NOW HE WILL TAKE A NIGHTLY JOURNEY ON THE WINGED DISC. HE WILL RETURN AT DAWN REFRESHED AND INSPIRED FOR HIS DAY'S WORK WITH HIS FELLOWS.

End of Rite.

"Cup of Tears"

INTRODUCTION TO CHAPTER 9
"TO TOUCH ONE HEART IS TO TOUCH THE WORLD."

My awareness of the need to bridge radiations between various religions and cultures came through a vivid vision I was given on the 18th of October, 1977. I found myself in a Temple, by the door, gazing at an altar at the far end. Behind the altar was a grey veil hanging in misty folds. On the altar was a metallic silver stag's head in profile facing left.

I was given instructions in a woman's voice: "Salute the altar." I bowed to the altar and the stag opened a dark eye. I had an impression that his right eye was golden. The stag shut his eye. I was told to move forward and repeat the salutation.

I did so saying: "I salute the altar." The eye again opened and I was reminded of the dark eyes of Pietas in Byzantine icons. Then it closed as before. I heard the mysterious voice again: "If you can bear it, do it for the third time." So once more I repeated the salutation and this time as the eye looked at me I felt awe-struck.

The eye closed and the mystical veil now showed forth women's white arms beckoning me forward. I drew closer, and a woman's voice asked me: "What is your intention?" And I felt she spoke from thousands of years in the past. I replied: "My intention is to bring into harmony the religion of Ancient Egypt and the Tradition of Avalon."

I felt that my intention was accepted.

When I receive a vision I always take care to wait for some inner guidance. It was many years before I travelled to Glastonbury after my brother Lawrence had passed into Spirit sphere. He had studied theology at Wells Cathedral.

In the late nineties I regularly visited crop circles, staying with my niece in Wiltshire. En route I would gladly take part in the Goddess Conference in Glastonbury – conveniently taking place during the crop circle season. I felt that Glastonbury was to be revered for its past, but I appreciated my yearly lessons in sacred geometry, with diagrams marked out on the fields round Silbury Hill and Avebury.

However, a member of the Fellowship of Isis in Wales suddenly changed my idea of Glastonbury only existing in the past. I was told of the remarkable connection between the West Country in England and our own countryside at the foot of Mount Leinster in Ireland. Our member told me that over the centuries, folk in Wales would assemble at the foot of the Preseli Hills to watch the full moon when it glided over the Blackstairs Range, including Mount Leinster – and then appear to sink into the Irish Sea. When this rare event occurred, there would surely be a total eclipse of the sun.

When our member talked to the oldest inhabitant of Preseli, she said that the place of the event was haunted by the White Lady, Bringer of Death. Clearly she was the moon who killed the sun with her shadow during their eclipse of the sun. The members of our Welsh Iseum watched the phenomenon during the most recent total eclipse of the sun late in the 20th Century. Therefore I felt sure that the knowledge of a forthcoming eclipse had been highly valued by our forebears. It explained why the early builders of Stonehenge made their earliest stone circle from blue stones drawn with intense labour from Preseli to Wiltshire.

This had me meditating as to the significance of mountains and hills. From the summit of Mount Leinster we can see the flash of the Irish Sea and the blue mountains of Preseli. Did our forebears signal from hills? Connections were important because of invasions. But I felt I had been given a deeper insight. What about pyramids? Many people seek a zodiac in the landscape around Glastonbury.

My own personal vision was extraordinary. Spiritually, in February 1989, I found myself in a dark corner of the Temple and from there emerged a Being of White Light. Startled, I did not invoke Pagan Deities – I found myself praying through the religion of my childhood. I tried the Lord's Prayer – nothing happened. The Being stood still. Then for no reason I called out the name "Michael". At once the Being responded with a leap of exultation! He put his arms around me like a rushing of wind – and then darted like a meteor through an indoor window in the direction of the High Altar of Isis! I had invoked and received the Archangel Michael.

I wondered what it was all about. I assumed it had to do with the inauguration of our new Noble Order of Tara. But why was he off to the

North-East and not to Egypt in the South?

It was in 2011 that I received my answer. I had decided that we had invoked the Goddesses so much that in England we had many Priestesses – but no men! At Clonegal Castle we did have Priests because my brother and I had worked together in equality as brother and sister. Men felt needed. So I suggested that wherever I visited in the British Isles in 2011 we should ask the FOI Priestesses of the local centre to invoke the God through a Priest. It was a huge success! We invoked Merlin in London and Lugh in a stone-age ruin – and Osiris in Southwark and by the Thames. We invoked the God Eros in the Glastonbury Goddess Conference with great popularity. But what could we do to equal Eros for our FOI gathering, with Irish members joining us?

What happened was unexpected and inspiring. In our meeting-place, our Irish Poet and Priest gave an Oracle of the Archangel Michael of Michael's Mount – the Tor. Michael explained that he never killed dragons. Yes, there was a dragon of energy beneath the Tor and certain other hills, coiled up below. Such coiled up serpents rotated like discs in an ever-moving spiral of interconnected circles. Above all, there was a mighty dragon of Divine energy within our own planet, guarded by the two Dragons of Magma. So all spiritual power was rooted in earth and if that power was misused our earth would fall, sterile, into a waste of dead craters. The time of renewal was at hand. Let us feel friendliness for all, knowing that from the tiniest lizard every snake has a very large grandmother! Let us honour and protect her and she will help us.

After this Oracle we Irish returned to Eire full of hope and joy.

CHAPTER 9: GLASTONBURY

ALCHEMICAL RITE
PART ONE: THE NARRATION
"WEEP! THE GODS WEEP WITH YOU!"

HOSTESS IN GLASTONBURY, GWENYTH VIVIENNE. SCENE IN A RUINED CHAPEL BY THE RIVER CAM. VISITANTS: PATH GUIDE: ELAINE. HELPER: AIDEN. ORACLE OF THE VISIONS: DEIRDRE.

ELAINE: Gwenyth, you have a prestigious career in the London Diplomatic Service. You have just bought this chapel, relic of the Reformation and this piece of land where you have planted apple trees. Why have you sent the Druid Clan of Dana an urgent plea for help?

GWENYTH: Because in Eire you have managed privately to keep your connection with the Nature Deities, the Sidhe. In Scotland and Wales the moralistic reformation has thrown out magic, sacraments, icons and any connection at all with Faeries, spirits, Deities and spirits of ancestors. I was brought up as a non-conformist in North Wales to believe that when you died you either went to heaven or hell, with no intermediate state or hope.

AIDEN: I was taught much the same thing in my liberal upbringing. Only we had no heaven or hell – just extinction when dead. Not a Deity or Faery existed – they were hallucinations brought on by madness or drugs. The first sign was to hear voices. The last sign was vision, and then you really were classified as clinically insane if you took these seriously.

ELAINE: I had the same sort of training. I found to safeguard my natural psychism I had to keep quiet about it. I only opened up when I met Aiden and others like us.

AIDEN: We used the safety camouflage "Bohemian". Artists were allowed to be eccentric. We could write and speak of Divinity – because this was "art" – therefore fiction.

ELAINE: It really seems we are giving the narration for Gwenyth!

GWENYTH: My experience has been far more than yours. I was brought up by my parents who were both ardent atheists. To them religion was a cast off remnant of evolution. Science showed us the correct modern way. They really did give me and my brother a good life. We had the best schools – my brother went to prep and public school and university, and I was sent to a co-educational establishment that insisted on the absolute equality of the sexes. They carried it to such extremes that we all wore trouser suits of the same shape and colour.

There was one fact that disturbed me. Yes, we were all of one sex – but it was masculine! We all had one religion – none. We all had the same moral code – none. We just obeyed the law of the land which our elders kept altering to suit themselves – we were Establishment. We could change things and we did.

We aimed for a unified population that was intelligent, with the same cultural way of life. Yes . . . And I found it profoundly dull.

There was a curious dichotomy in my life. For during the day I worked in caring for abused women and children – but in the evening I took off my worn working clothes and changed into smart clothes with appropriate jewellery. "Breaking boundaries" in my social world referred to cricket. "Appropriate" had a sinister meaning in my work and "Boundaries" in Care Work did not apply to cricket. Disraeli once said that in England there were two nations – the rich and the poor. Now there were two different types of humans: Those who could control computers and the millions who were ruled by them. Through computers they were fed or let starve, be taken into care or left to be abused. As long as I filled in forms I needed no conscience. Everything was filed.

ELAINE: We read of such happenings every day. Humans are evolving into machines and live virtual lives.

GWENYTH: But people cannot live on virtual food and drink. This I found out in a terrible way. It was a bright day in October and I planned to meet some well-thought of scientists at a dinner-party in Knightsbridge. I would wear a sophisticated black dress and do my hair up to show my new opal earrings. That morning I was visiting a Care Home for elderly women and felt pretty exhausted. I work long hours. As I left the final ward I heard someone call me in a weak voice. Impatiently I turned round. At the end bed was an old woman. I don't remember having noticed her before. Now she was leaning out of her bed, her right arm stretched frantically towards a cup on her locker. Her mauve dried lips were moving but she could not reach the cup. I decided to give it to her, but it only contained an old used teabag.

The woman was dehydrated. I felt icy cold. She had fallen back on her pillow and lay motionless, still gazing at the cup. I sent for a Doctor as an emergency. Meanwhile I sat on her bed, my legs shaking. I feared she was dying of thirst.

I found that I was copying the woman by also staring at the cup. It began to change. It looked smaller and made of some organic material, like a segment of a cow's horn. It had over it a small lid and I found myself thinking: "That's to keep off flies!" I was in shock as I was violently struck by a glowing fire in my heart. I knew what the cup was. It was the Holy Grael!

I was overcome by weeping shaking my whole body. I wept aloud like an Irish widow keening. I wept for the old woman and for my own dead mother and for all I knew who suffered from cancer and abuse and fear of pain and death. I was unable to stop. People were beginning to stare at me.

As I wept I rose above the earth and gazed at the pale face of the moon shining like a silver orb through the cup. I saw a Fairy Thorn which was warmed by a dragon's fiery breath in the centre of the earth. The tree was nourished by the watery atmosphere. Its white flowers were the stars. I entered ecstasy.

Suddenly a doctor was touching me on the shoulder. He said "I am told you are the patient's Care Worker. You need a rest. I too have drawn water from the Well of Tears at the World's End. Go to Glastonbury. There you will find your true Vocation as I did." When I rose to my feet and looked around, the Doctor was nowhere to be seen. In his place a brisk younger Doctor with his iPad came up and said: "I will take charge now."

And so now I seek for the Bliss I found when I saw the Holy Grael in the hospital. Here I am in Glastonbury where the Doctor said I should visit. Yet I have found nothing spiritual in the famous tourist sites. I must discover the True Grael again. Can you help me?

DEIRDRE: To accomplish this I am told from Spirit that we need to invoke the Cailleach, She Who Weeps.

ELAINE: At dawn we shall assemble in this Chapel, which is not as ruined as it appears.

PART TWO: ALCHEMICAL RITE
THE MYSTICAL ISLE OF AVALON
"WHERE YOUR HEART IS, THERE IS YOUR HOME."

IN A RUINED CHAPEL IN GLASTONBURY THE ALCHEMICAL PARTICIPANTS ARE ASSEMBLED.

THE CHAPEL LOOKS GLORIOUS WITH SILKEN BANNERS PAINTED BY MEMBERS SHOWING CELTIC GODDESSES AND GODS, AND THE AIR IS RICH WITH INCENSE. THIRTEEN CANDLES ARE LIGHTED. IN THE NORTH, IN A SHADOWED RECESS, LIES DEIRDRE OF THE VISIONS IN TRANCE. SHE IS COVERED WITH A MISTY VEIL. AIDEN IS IN FULL ROBES WITH HIGH MITRE OF MANANNAN OF THE OCEANS.

AIDEN: I invoke the God Manannan Mac Lir, Son of Lir of Space, Deity of the Mighty Oceans and All Waters, right down to the smallest teardrop shed by a little monkey in fear of vivisection in a laboratory.

ELAINE *(ROBED IN THE VIOLET AND BLUE OF THE MORRIGAN)*: In the sacred Name of the Morrigan, Maiden, Queen, Cailleach, the Widow, I pray for the Oracle of An Cailleach, She Who Weeps. I pray for the lost, the lonely, and the abused.

ORACLE OF AN CAILLEACH, THE WISE ONE

Rather should you pray for the abusers! For every small child tormented by the stupidity and egotism of elders is blessed in the Spirit Realm. Each victim is welcomed by the Sidhe of earth, air, fire and water, and by those humans who have longed for children and yet been denied them on earth.

But the abusers find themselves once more bound to Manannan's Wheel of fatal cause and effect. In the circling of the zodiac, all that has been done for good or evil bears fruit in many lives of lost souls, either on earth, or in other planets. It is they who need help.

In the revolving spiral of time and space, I manifest as Youth and Creator and Wise Woman. And so does my Consort Manannan. To attain the Great Awakening which all seek, first blindly, then with passion, you need to place yourself in the centre of the Wheel of your Destiny. Then you will rise above the wasteland of cruelty and stupidity and see that each being on earth has chosen an individual path. Finally each being attains the Centre of Reality that seems so far * * * and yet is under your own feet!

AIDEN: We give thanks to the Goddess An Cailleach for Her Wisdom.

ELAINE *(TO GWENYTH)*: I shall be your Guide in this mystical Labyrinth of the Wheel if you accept me. If so, tell me what you truly desire!

GWENYTH: I have a life-long nostalgia for the lost island of Avalon for its charming inhabitants, who do not show themselves to me. I would give my life to reach the Land of Heart's Desire.

GWENYTH IS LED TO A COUCH BEFORE A LIGHTED ALTAR. SHE IS ALREADY HALF IN TRANCE AND IS TOLD TO KEEP ENOUGH CONSCIOUSNESS TO GIVE THE COMPANY HER REPORT.

TRANCE JOURNEY

GWENYTH: This is so beautiful! At last I have Vision. It is just what I have always dreamed of. My hair hangs down and I am wearing a robe of blue that is fluttering in a soft breeze. Oh, I could rest here! Perfect youths and maidens are in the distance, like a Pre-Raphaelite painting – so that is what artists saw in visions! And now I can see. They are floating on a shining river in a boat – there are other boats in the distance and to my joy they are sailing towards a mysterious island half hidden by mist.

A small group beckons me to a gilded boat with purple perfumed sails. Usually I don't like bank holiday crowds with jolly people showing their teeth in silly laughter. I like these people. It must be the future, when everyone will be cultivated and have perfect bodies – no obesity. They have a sweet seriousness and can read my thought.

"Come with us, Vivienne," says a maiden with long golden plaits. "Your time has come." Suddenly I feel doubtful. Shall I go or stay and have a well-earned rest?

I know that if I lose this opportunity to travel into the unknown, it will never occur again and I shall live a quiet but uninteresting life. So I get into the boat – it glides swiftly and I become aware of swans flying in a V formation above. I feel vaguely holy, like a Burne-Jones angel, with "Lohengrin" music – yes, I too come from distant lands where shines the Holy Grael – I am getting sleepier and notice we all have reddish hair – why did that girl call me by my second name, Vivienne? Wasn't she a witch?

I decide not to risk this voyage – I try to get out of the boat – but the maidens hold me with jewelled arms.

As our boat approaches the lovely beach of the Island, fringed by oak, apple and thorn trees – there is a sudden gale that bends the trees. I am whirled below into the sea and find I am drowning. Frantically I reach for help but my hand is caught in a tangle of red hair. I drag myself free – it is only seaweed – and find I am sinking into an underground cave. So here I shall find the Well of the Mysteries. I surrender myself with faith.

I have never been so shocked! I am not in the depths of the mystical Isle of Avalon. This is not sacred at all. I am precipitated into the dinner-party which I had rejected after my Grael vision. The scientists and writers are seated around an oak dinner table with placemats. On the walls are oil paintings of distinguished persons. "So here is our latest Avalonian Dreamer," says a clever looking man with a beard.

An elderly woman in the robe of a University Professor looks me up and down and says: "She has not had the time to change into her latest black model gown. But she still wears her opal earrings. One would expect that."

A plump lady with red hair takes off her shawl and puts it round me. "Don't mind them," she says in a warm voice. "You know they like holding forth on metaphysics, and you enjoy listening to them. A perfect arrangement."

To my intense relief my own Doctor – the one who told me to find the Well speaks. But my heart sinks at his words. "She did not weep for the old lady," he says, "but for herself. Her overwhelming guilt was to be exposed. We see now why the word 'charity' was dropped in favour of 'Care'. They'll have to find another word now. 'Care' means 'cruel'."

I burst out: "You are as bad. Why don't you talk *to* me and not *about* me while I stand here?"

"Was this not your method?" asks the Doctor. "You were the Dominant and 'the patient' was the Subject."

Despite myself I begin to be interested. "You can apply this Dominant and Subject to empires and states." I say. "And to families . . . babies are blocked by the dominant culture, and are blocked into submission. As humans we have power of life and death over our 'pets'. Humans are the tyrants of all nature."

Again this strange swirling motion overcomes me, as if a mighty wind is tearing across the dinner-party. "I won't stay here and endure bullying," I say, "even if you rule the Establishment with your power."

I am struck by Lightening. White light strikes my forehead – I have a star in my head. The dizzy swirling slows down and I am above the earth. In the centre is a hill and round it a strange landscape is rotating. I find the Doctor is standing by me. This time he is not in a dinner-jacket but wears a white Druid robe. He says "Many call me Merlin. I have many names on many planets. I meet the pilgrims at the Threshold when they dare attain a wider consciousness."

I ask: "What is this landscape that I see below us?" Merlin says: "You see around us the true pattern of space and time, ever changing with the pulse of life. Here is the real Glastonbury with its Michael's Mount. Around is the pattern of the land going back through the ages – from iron to space age. What I wish to show you is the path of human revolution and the destiny which is already there in Divine reality. Now your heart centre is awakened, you need to beware of obsession, which can delay your Awakening."

"What obsession?" I ask. "Tell me and I will avoid it." Merlin laughs. "Ah- if it were only that easy, all suffering and evil would be seen for what it is - self delusion, created by ourselves. For instance, I will show you pictures of this land and see if you are in danger of identifying with the transient and so losing eternity."

I find myself alone in a vast weeping crowd. We are at the foot of the Tor. The people look pretty poor with shabby home-made clothes and I notice their bad teeth. Why are they weeping? Then more important people arrive on horseback or carriages. They have a feeling of power and the people shrink away from them. I am about to witness an execution. A quiet man is taken forward and I watch his death after such horrible torture that I shut my eyes. I know who he is – the Abbot of Glastonbury. I keep telling myself this is only history. I feel profound sorrow.

The scene changes, but the story is the same. I see primitive people offering human sacrifice to the Gods. The Gods look on. The human indifference to suffering I witness in later centuries, in their acceptance of the slave trade by otherwise kindly families who have decided that they can do nothing to stop it, in fear of losing their livelihoods if they speak out. And I think: "I always liked those I took to be good natured, kindly people, but now I despise them. They won't jeopardise their comfortable lives by intervening and so angering their neighbours."

Two centuries later I see a city being bombed. I know it is Bristol. Its centre is flattened out. People, animals and buildings are reduced to dust. I recognise the same Gods and Goddesses as before, calmly looking on. And I begin to see the connection. As we sow, so do we reap. This is the Law. If the Deities were to intervene, they would also be Dominants ruling over human subjection.

Then to the dying wailing of an air-raid siren, I find I am whirling through the labyrinth of time and space again – back to Merlin and the hilltop. "You have passed the Test," he says. "You have faced the truth. The Gods only intervene when inspired by the Divine Spirit. Although you hate evil, you care for people and animals whether they behave well or badly. You maintain the balance of your work for true Charity through feeling and honesty of mind. Your sense of humour saves your sanity."

"Why then do I need help from these Alchemists?" I ask. Merlin replies: "Because, although you are balanced, you lack inspiration, the White Dove of the Divine Spirit. Without Divinity you are exiled from Eternity. Eternity is not infinite length. It is Now."

I find I am rising above Avalon and the planet earth and I become aware of our starry galaxy. Through the Tor and all other sacred hills on earth are connected with the great channel leading to the spiritual centre of the galaxy.

So what do I *truly* want? I only want to know how I can help the old woman I neglected. I am back in the dinner-party. Merlin stands by me and the members are collected at a round table and on it are glasses and cups, some valuable and some cheap. A tall stately woman addresses me. "This is the Feast of the Gods," she said "and all may partake." I look round. Here is Manannan and Grainne, and Cerridwen and Taliesin – and I recognise famous artists and poets, and those who are great but unknown to fame.

"Your true prayer is heard," says the Lady, and she rises into celestial heights, surrounded by the stars. "I am the old woman in the bed, An Cailleach, She Who Weeps. Give me to drink of the Grael, and you will forgive yourself." She lifts her right arm and it becomes the withered arm of the old woman. I am once more in the Care Home. She is reaching towards the cup. I know what to do. I reach for the cup and I pick out the teabag, now sodden with my tears. I gently ease the old lady back onto the pillow and I squeeze the strong tea upon her dry lips. She smiles and then she falls asleep.

GWENYTH VIVIENNE SLOWLY RETURNS FROM TRANCE. THE LINES OF CARE ON HER FACE HAVE VANISHED. SHE SMILES AND JOINS IN THE THANKS TO THE DEITIES. THE COMPANY SHARES REPORTS.

GWENYTH: I have found that She Who Weeps also smiles.

End of Rite.

"Leesa and Mwe"

INTRODUCTION TO CHAPTER 10
"WE ARE WANDERERS IN SEARCH OF OUR LOST HEAVEN."

It was on a misty Bank Holiday weekend – Sunday morning in June 2013, when a strange happening brought my recent problems and speculations to an end. I was totally astonished – bewildered – at a new beginning. It was so strange and wonderful that I wish to share the experience with everyone.

It began this way. The Castle grounds had been full of delightful wedding guests who had shared in some blessing in each part of the grounds, to make romantic a registry office marriage. That morning I decided "to feel the vibes" left behind by these visitors, lovely young people with lots of flowers.

Now I was practising adjusting to stray people wandering round our gardens, where before there had been none – just wood pigeons cooing. I am a solitary stroller but felt guided to be friendly with every sort of visitor. I was feeling very down to earth, in jersey and trousers.

I spoke briefly to one or two strollers in our wilderness, where there is a lake with an island, which borders the River of the Oak, the River Derry – the Daire. For instance I met a tall fair woman who cooked at the neighbouring hotel, and I said that she was very welcome to come at any time. She commented on the peace and tranquility. I was now on the bank of the lake and saw someone else. I was a bit surprised at finding quite so many stray tourists after eleven on a Sunday. Most people slept late.

Then I saw further on the path a very tall man wearing a long black cloak to his feet - with a hood – I'm not sure whether it was up or not, and I think it was lined with crimson. I thought "Good – I can have another nice chat," and I called out "It's good to see people walking here!" or words to that effect. The man came straight towards me – to a few feet away. Then his cloak billowed out towards the lake and a huge oak tree – and to my amazement he vanished by the tree. I felt a silvery-shining tinkling all over my head.

I call him "The Wanderer." He had the dignity of some mysterious King – a Shaman. I feel I would not have seen him if I had not been friendly to all solitary wanderers. I wonder what this apparition bodes. I know he had Divine regality.

When we align ourselves with Golden Flow, life becomes meaningful and blissful, whatever happens in the world. We who keep in touch with our souls gain that lovely communion with Spirit World. What we enjoy is Vocation, so we know when we journey in this planetary labyrinth. I know that I am grateful that this happened – in broad daylight – supplementing my usual visions and teachings which come at dawn when I am half in my soul body – and it can be hard to come back.

A Druid told me that before 2012 he and fellow Druids unblocked a tunnel leading to the inner realm beneath Glastonbury Tor, and hence to Galactic Centre. Our Temple was "unblocked" late in February. Many psychics say it has completely changed and brightened – there was a silver-white flow through the window above the Well and brilliant warm colours from the earth. Welling from the High Altar and the two pillars before it, is a source of fire and black power which turns into vivid and beautiful rainbow colours from The Mothers. My brother Lawrence described both. I speculate that the white power over the Well is of Isis, and is of air, breath, and the flow in our bodies through the cerebral-spinal system. The power beneath our Cave of the Mothers is gold power and flows through the blood, the sympathetic nervous system, and relates to Ra. The union of these two forms create gold and silver orbs of power – chakras of power.

Power energy may not be seen as Divine but rather as power that translates this energy to the Divine purpose. Terrible cruelty and violence comes from misusing this power.

The intention of the Fellowship is to unite the Divine Source, Love and Truth in harmony. We try to unite these two Divine attributers in the Holy of Holies, the Star Chapel, with no outside walls. Ishtar and Tammuz, Isis and Osiris, Vishnu and Lakshmi, Maria and Christ, bring this wholeness now fragmented on this earth. We fight subjection, domination, exploitation of humans, animals, birds, fish, reptiles and insects of every species – all creatures of the Mother's sacred elements.

I paraphrase Katherine Tynan's poem "The New Jerusalem" ... I stand before our Sun and Moon Gate, leading to our Well of Truth, and say:

> *"The Temple of Isis is Holy;*
> *Her Gate is open wide;*
> *All She calls may enter; No seeker is denied."*

CHAPTER 10: ZIMBABWE

ALCHEMICAL RITE
PART ONE: THE NARRATION
"TWO PEOPLE LEAVE EACH OTHER IN OPPOSITE DIRECTIONS. THEY CIRCULATE THE EARTH. THEY MEET."

HOSTESS AND HOST IN ZIMBABWE, HENRY MWE AND JANE LEESA. SCENE IN A CIRCLE OF TREES AND STONES. IN A REMOTE VALLEY NEAR RUTENGA BY THE RIVER MWENEZI. VISITANTS: PATH GUIDE: AIDEN. HELPER: ELAINE. ORACLE AND VISIONARY: DEIRDRE.

AIDEN: Henry and Jane, you have sent a message for urgent alchemical healing for a disastrous situation. Yet you are seated here calmly, with African instruments and carved figures. Henry, you wear European dress, Jane you are in African clothing.

HENRY: Ah – we long to be like you two, twin souls, in harmony. We would prefer to tell each our own story as to our desolate situation. We are poles apart.

DEIRDRE: You'll only receive one Oracle, I feel guided to tell, from no less than the All Mother, Nana Buluku.

ELAINE: Who will give the narration first? Henry?

HENRY: Not as my life is worth! Jane would immediately say I was putting myself in the dominant role of male supremacy. Already she resents the name "Jane".

JANE: Let me speak for myself. As the victim role is pushed upon to me as an aggressive feminist, I shall submit.

ELAINE: This should be most interesting. What are you if not "Jane"?

JANE: I am African. My true African name is Leesa, which I found in one of your African ceremonies. This is a useful ritual, counteracting what I was brain-washed with when in the mission school I was "charitably" educated. They called me Jane. I notice the boy "Mwe' in your rite fitted in very easily to be called "Henry".

HENRY: I aim to win power by learning the white man's sciences – not just to protest uselessly like Jane.

AIDEN: This is Jane's narration. Leesa, please continue.

JANE LEESA: This was a typically "natives" educational establishment. They gave us no powers to make money or love – no powers. We were blocked in every passion, especially we women. They put us in long shapeless garments called "Mother Hubbards" to cover bare breasts.

HENRY: If they had not – you would step out of their classroom and you would have been raped in exactly four minutes.

AIDEN: Henry, please don't interrupt. Your turn will come.

LEESA: I was deprived of all that makes a true woman – our African religion.

HENRY: We haven't got one. Not a valid one.

LEESA: Our religion is based on nature and lost tribal customs. I longed to be taught the language of drums – not a stupid catechism. The only book I liked was Shaw's "Black Girl in search of God." She found Voltaire – that was all. But I delved into my natural psychic ability – that exists in nearly everyone if it hadn't been cauterized by mental rules and regulations.

ELAINE: How on earth did you come to work with Henry?

LEESA: You can call it a dynamic occultism partnership.

HENRY: More like a continual sectarian civil war.

AIDEN: What help do you want and would both accept?

LEESA: I cannot continue with this perpetual conflict of our beliefs – or rather his lack of any – and my feelings. I lie awake feeling hatred that has no outlet. I suppose you call such a relationship "love" – though I cannot communicate with Mwe on any heart level. He makes silly jokes or clever remarks if I tell him my heart's longings.

HENRY: As these consist of day dreaming for some divine man from heaven or UFO, some mysterious stranger of indefinable superiority to human men! Such a being leads her to wandering by the sea shore, hair down, longing for a man from the stars. In the old days I suppose it would have been some God or angel. But what I suspect – this is a danger in our evolution. I read a book by H.G. Wells on the fear of this danger. It's called "Star Begotten". She hopes for a Super-child as in Bethlehem, an Indigo, a star baby who will supersede me. But this shall not happen. She has very little practical brains. We use chemicals to check weird children.

No. I despise her childish dreams, her talk of psyche and souls, and the like, beyond physical, organic form. She needn't think I despise the Goddess. I respect the Mother of All.

I too have my dreams of the modern woman, very tall with long, long boyish legs, and a sense of humour, which is more than Leesa has, and a Degree in Western science. It is practical. Western scientists and financiers rule the world. And I want to rule the world, preferably in the United States! You may wonder at our partnership. However, there is an area I am deficient in – it is Jane who has psychic powers, though I am sure scientists will find an explanation for such phenomena. There is one reason we stay together, and I cannot explain this. I love her.

LEESA: Yes, it's funny, you madden me, but I am in love with you too!

DEIRDRE: Using my despised female psychic ability, I can see plainly your aura class. Leesa's aura is a sort of fluffy pink, and Henry's is an orderly indigo.

LEESA: What do you propose to do about it. He's all mind and I know I'm all feeling. Capricorn versus Pisces. Earth versus Air.

HENRY: Astrology is nonsense. Ask any astronomer . . .

ELAINE: To answer your question Leesa, as to what we propose to do. I should like to explain to both of you how spiritual alchemy works. It is a basic spiritual truth to true Alchemists that there is only Divine Energy in the cosmos from star to atom. The One Eternal Being and Holy Reality to this energy is Deity. Deity contains both ethics and goodness in time and place, so everything has really happened. Change comes through time and evolution of consciousness, becoming aware of this reality. Divine Energy is perfect in each individual snowflake and in each star. Therefore there is no hierarchy of importance; for God the Divine is all present in time and space. Nothing is lost. Evil is transmuted by the Mother's love and wisdom.

HENRY: That sounds good but how do people evolve if it is all there?

AIDEN: As this evolution expands, the wider the area that is comprehended, the greater and nobler the extension through many lives and states of a being. A true alchemist knows what is going to happen by remembering what DID happen. Only the virtues of Love, Beauty and Truth are eternal. The rest – evil – vanishes when it is recognised.

LEESA: How about our feelings of individuality – our emotions?

ELAINE: Without the humblest creature born of the Mother, the Divine Being would be incomplete. Think of it all as a vast Persian carpet, our many life paths. We only see a tiny part of the carpet - as seen by those in Plato's Cave in Greek philosophy. "All the world's a stage" says Shakespeare. We choose to play in various dramas. Every folk story or fairy tale has deeper meaning. Shamans show the starry heavens as a picture book. We identify with Hercules – Ariadne – these adventures teach us our own lives are projections into the wonderful eternal divine pattern.

LEESA: I often have the feeling it's all happened . . . That we are here working through the mystery of the Unseen Lover. So many myths are telling us our inner longings.

HENRY: This does explain why people adore epics and operas and paintings and stories. We are buying into the dramas of our own story. The Gods are really our teachers who know more than us and are teachers of the Arts.

AIDEN: But we can also help the teachers remember it. Deities still speak to humans who will listen and always have through Oracles, through the world religions. Let us invoke such an African Wise One, the Mother Goddess Nana Buluku.

ELAINE: Let us gather at dawn as the sun rises, here by the Holy River Mwenezi . . .

PART TWO: ALCHEMICAL RITE

DEIRDRE LIES ON A MANY COLOURED SARONG ON GRASS AT DAWN, AROUND HER ARE AIDEN, ELAINE, HENRY AND LEESA.

AIDEN: On the wide circling earth, on all the myriad earths and shining stars, you preside, the All Mother, Nana Buluku. Bestow on us your Oracle.

ORACLE OF THE GODDESS NANA BULUKU

We who are Mothers know the secret of every heart. For this cosmos is not made of only an interlocked grid of far-seeing shamans and thousands of strange creatures in every kind of earth. Wonderful as are coloured stones and richly filled oceans and towering trees, and the brightly patterned sky with planet encircling stars, there is nothing more creative and wonderful than hidden dreams! Within every heart, whether it is the crawling hairy caterpillar or the flying bats at night – within each is the hidden longing for the Other.

A butterfly seeks the mysterious stranger as do the roaring animals in the African jungles. The atom seeks its small solar system as keenly as does a sun looking for its dark haven within a galactic black hole. A black hole leads each sun to Heaven as certainly as a baby longs to be born from within the dark womb.

There is now boredom in the cosmos. There is all art, music, architecture, that enshrines the omnipresent goal, the ideal – a lovely person in a garden – the avatar – is incomplete each without the Other. Without the Other the most powerful life is meaningless.

When you find joy, love, vision, truth – share it with the Others. Then what you love with will increase infinitely, for the Other is the Divinity you lack. Perfection is your goal – through the Others. There is your hidden Gold.

ELAINE: We give thanks for this Oracle, given to us through the dedication of our Visionary.

AIDEN: Henry, I will be your Path Guide, if you accept me. Lie on this couch and enter trance state.

HENRY: I am well read in occultism. This is a form of hypnotism. I expect that's it. I feel, rather sleepy.

HENRY LIES ON COUCH AND SHUTS HIS EYE, OR RATHER ONE EYE. THE OTHER IS WATCHING AIDEN.

AIDEN: Both eyes.

HENRY: Oh, all right. This is a scientific experiment. I choose to cooperate.

AIDEN: Good. You are sleepy.

TRANCE JOURNEY

AIDEN: Henry, what can you see with your eyes shut.

HENRY: OK. But I just want to say about all this Other business, the Other should be attractive. Don't produce various ethical virtues and a plain woman, or people. I choose my Others. They must have brains. Intellectual.

AIDEN: Ah, we've provided them all right. They are as attractive and intellectual . . . They are in the room in which you find yourself . . . by the way, this is not hypnosis. It is the most powerful projection known.

HENRY: You're right there. Your technique is brilliant. The room is real.

AIDEN: Give us an accurate report of what you experience.

HENRY: I'm in what looks like a very up-to-date laboratory. Just the sort of place we need in Africa. And surely here at last are the scientific Western Others. There is one rather plain woman who is arguing against some experiment she calls cruel and unnecessary. Curious. I like controversy. Yet not one of them looks at me. Why? Then I look down. I have hairy legs. Outrageous! What has happened? Is this a real projection? I have thin hairy legs with monkey feet. And I'm *imprisoned* in a cage. Remove this projection at once!

ELAINE: Once the projection is validified – it's valid. You must finish it. You are a primate. Rather a fine one, doubtless attractive to monkey Others.

HENRY: I still have my intelligence. This is one of those occult tests they tell of, to access my intelligence. Darwinism. I have to release myself from this humiliating form by proving to these scientists that I am their equal. I try to get their attention by rattling on the bars in semaphore. They begin to stare. Then I begin talking to them. I say I am a human being, a university graduate, and appear to be undergoing an occult initiation. Give me some paper and I will prove I know differential calculus.

At least that is what I mean. But it comes out in monkey chatter. I try to impress them by meaningful gestures. I have at last made some impression. . . The woman defends me.

"Isn't he sweet? I suppose you will go through with the experiment." A young man near her says "I don't care for experiments on primates. But I was convinced by the argument that this may benefit thousands of people through the proposed inoculation. Also he's cost a huge amount."

An elderly man says "I'm sick of this bleeding heart business of the anti-vivisection lobby. They ought to think of dying human-beings. Let's begin shortly."

They wheel my cage into a smaller room filled with terrifying instruments that make me think of the Spanish Inquisition. Suddenly black fear overcomes me. I am terrified of torture. One of them asks. "Do we give an anaesthetic?"

Another man says: "They could make the findings inconclusive. There must be no contamination with chemicals."

I shake the bars of my cage and begin to scream. I cannot imagine any human would be as anguished and cry like this. My hot tears splash my face.

The woman who was against the experiment tries to persuade them again. "Can't you see he is absolutely terrified?" Again they speak of human needs. She is so repelled that they threaten to make a gagging order on the spot if she "whistle blows" in opposition, reporting them for cruelty to animals. She will be black-listed in her career, and lose her considerable pension.

It's strange. *I can look into her mind.* She realises the only way she can stop this torture is to kill me. She has no care for her career and pension. She knows what is right. She says to me: "My poor friend, go to a better world." And she plunges her poisonous syringe into my arm.

HENRY RETURNS FROM TRANCE WITH A JERK, AND SITS BOLT UPRIGHT.

From now on, call me Mwe! Now are you going to get Leesa to project too?

ELAINE *(LAUGHS)*: Leesa has had her trance. She projected into your drama through her telepathic gift – she has empathy.

LEESA: Mwe, I love you. What I hope for is that you will bring all your scientific know-how to our joint dream of building the Rainbow Paradise of Nana Buluku, Ile Ise, the House of Light.

REPORTS ARE SHARED AND THANKS GIVEN TO THE DEITIES. RAYS OF HARMONY ARE SENT FORTH.

End of Rite.

Sources: "The Sayings of the Ancient One: Wisdom From Ancient Africa," P.G. Bowen, Theosophical Publishing House. "Teachings of the Great Berber philosopher, Maylo Meya." "Traditions of the Yuruba Tribe of Zimbabwe." "The Adventures of the Black girl in her Search for God," George Bernard Shaw, Constable & Robinson. "The Secret School: Preparation for Contact", Whitley Strieber.

"Mask of the Medusa"

PREFACE TO CHAPTER 11
"THE MEDUSA LABYRINTH TRIAL"

The Gods enjoy the task of moving humanity from one to another of the four aeons, the Kabbalistic Zohar, each spanning roughly five thousand years. Their goal was to move us from the Carthaginian and Cretan aeon of Taurus to the realm of Athena – elegant aeon of Pisces and Greek culture.

The plan was that of the constellation of Taurus. The centre and goal was the sigil, of Aldebaron, the Red Star, the Bullseye, principal star of Taurus. It was protected fiercely by the Double Axe of Crete, the waxing and waning moon of the Goddess Passiphae, mother of Ariadne, with her four snakes.

However, the star Venus, of Taurus was the Eight-Pointed Star that encouraged the pilgrims. So the brave neophyte entered the path of balance, of choice between the loving rays of Venus, and the severe power of the moon, and Minos, the Bull King. Theseus found his way to the centre, guided by Ariadne, but he deserted her, and got entrapped as punishment by the Queen, Passiphae.

Ariadne chose the God Bacchus to enliven the age of Pisces, which ever since was guided by him. Pisces was a duel sign caught between Rome and Athens – Venus and Athena. You are the neophyte. You have to choose. We have been between the passions of religious wars, and the rise of modern science. We are now faced with a great change from Pisces, the wasteland of the Fisher King, to the on-rushing waters of the Age of Aquarius, from the depths of the Earth to the clouds of Heaven pouring water from the Holy Grail of the Divine Spirit guided by the twins Isis and Osiris, inspiring all beings and elements.

INTRODUCTION TO CHAPTER 11

"IT'S A LONG WAY TO TIPPERARY.
(BUT OUR HEARTS ARE ALWAYS THERE.)"

Yes, it's a long way to what we as children knew as the Great War. We all sang this cheery ditty. Even in 1925 it was relevant. Every day, we could pack up our troubles in our old kit bags, and smile, while millions had died. Nanny said the Germans were poisoning our ice cream, but Daddy said "don't believe her – she thinks the moon is made of green cheese!" I was discovering a grown-up World of Lies.

It seemed a great hoax was created by people who had their own agenda, who persuaded people to give their lives for the paradise of Tipperary, but sacrificed themselves to the God Moloch, and ended up dead on barbed wire in somewhere called No Man's Land. Truly, it belonged to No Man. It belonged to death. Seen through childish eyes, the God of Death had a black moustache. He was called Lord Kitchener, and summoned you to die for King and Country. Then he changed from God to Devil – De Valera, and he wore horn-rimmed spectacles and presided over burning buildings in Dublin, where to my alarm, I was going to live! Later this God of Death grew a huge chin, and was called Mussolini, and dropped bombs on black people who had no defence. Suddenly, he shrank, and grew a little square moustache, and became God the Leader - Hitler. His moustache dramatically changed into a huge handlebar one, and he became the Steel God - Stalin. Both Gods had millions of people exterminated in labour camps. The Steel God, was followed by many of my student friends, the God the Leader had older spiritual devotees who followed occult ideas.

I didn't. As a three-month old baby, I had seen God. I didn't worship him. I just liked him. He had no hair at all; He looked Tibetan, and was surrounded by brilliant blue light. I was saved from being a Catholic or Protestant, Green or Orange, and so the Civil War, by other Gods and Goddesses - Beings of Light, who shared their Goodness and Wisdom. Now I am ninety-six. How can I warn people to escape from those who use our energy to mis-use power in the names of the Gods and Goddesses? Heaven is truly around us. Let us make it our home now!

My Teachers taught me think-feel language. It is very easy. It is spiritual language. They never humiliated or criticised me in front of others. They did not get me to blame my parents or others or the way I was brought up. They taught me to have empathy with all creatures. They were enormously powerful, and could perform miracles. How? Their sphere of being controlled our time and space. They were eternal, not subject to death; they could talk to my ancestors. They knew the future, because it is already marked out in their time maps. So they could help me to grow up, and to rise above fear of death, to recognise evil and so dissolve it. These things exist only at our limited level. I had to learn to choose good and reject evil, because good is Real, and evil is a waste of Reality.

We have the Divine in us; it is part of the Alchemical Flow. Dusk and dawn are the best time to contact the two worlds of matter and spirit. You will sing with the blackbird who sang in Flanders field so long ago. We can enter the Labyrinth of Time and Space; the Labyrinth of Stars that lead us to the Centre of All.

CHAPTER 11: CRETE
"THE MIRAGE OF DECEPTION."

A VISION QUEST
PART ONE: THE NARRATION
"EVERY STEP MATTERS:
THE TRUE SHAMAN DOES NOT LOSE SIGHT OF HIS GOAL."

THE RESIDENT GOD IS MINOS, THE TWO-FACED BULL, PAINTED IN A SMALL PRIVATE TEMPLE NEAR KNOSSOS. VISITANTS: NARRATOR AND NEOPHYTE, PERCY. ARIADNE, ELAINE. LUCIFER-HERMES, AIDEN. ORACLE, DEIRDRE. SET-EROS, LOCAL FOI PRIEST. ALCHEMICAL FOI GROUP.

ELAINE *(TO PERCY)*: You beg for initiation of the Labyrinth by Ariadne. You say the situation is desperate. Why?

PERCY: You have not penetrated my esoteric disguise. I am the poet Shelley, come back to have the Supreme Awakening.

ELAINE: I see. May I be Ariadne?

PERCY: No. My tiresome wife drowned herself. I think it's her fault I failed the initiation, though Byron gave a nice funeral oration by the sea. You see the sea did not take me. I just stood there like an ass frozen with terror.

ELAINE: As a Guide, I am going to be your second intellectual wife, who wrote the Frankenstein horror story. The first wife was just silly. The second was unscrupulous and took you off by cunning. She will be a good Ariadne, teller of tales of the Jekyll and Hyde dual personality.

AIDEN: I want a good part. I will be both mad scientist Frankenstein and the monster.

DEIRDRE: We see the compulsive magic of Greek mysteries. We are all involved. Let me speak.

AIDEN: So it is. You have the right of choice.

PERCY: As you gather, I am still a neo-romantic. These days I belong to the Golden Dawn, and have been filmed acting in one of their secret rituals for Facebook. I was the Imperator like Yeats. My hair curled round my mask and black hood. It is glorious that Byron is with us as romantic as ever - one of the Officers. He is busy re-doing the Wagner Ring cycle, to make it politically correct. How on earth can you do that?

PRIEST: It is beyond you! You are not an initiate!

PERCY: How can I become an initiate?

PRIEST: By joining the Fellowship of Isis that is especially suited to naïve idealists. You are taken in by everyone. Your father is an Earl, and you are rich. You always tell every secret you hear, and FOI has no secrets so you won't be punished for divulging! FOI is for psychic people like A.E. and yourself. Yeats and I were not psychic so we needed secrecy and the occult to give us status.

PERCY: So here I am, ready for any trial or ordeal you have lined up.

ELAINE: We don't give ordeals. We don't try people. Only life itself works through the Law of Balance. Every action has an equal and opposite reaction. It is the Law of Fate, ordained by the Divine Mother, who insists on all her children being saved. And so they are, by Grace if not by Virtue.

AIDEN: Life is its own antidote. Birth vs. Death, Matter vs. Spirit. We teach how to control Cause and Effect through the Labyrinth which the Deities created for the Cretans, the last of the Atlantean colonists. It kept their ancient ways. They are so old fashioned after being submerged!

DEIRDRE: Let us meet this evening and bathe in the light of the moon by the sea.

PART TWO:
DISSOLUTION OF THE MIRAGE OF DECEPTION.

DEIRDRE: Friends! The Great Hoax, created by Pallas Athena and Minos as a Path of Learning – a vision quest - a shaman journey. To look in the Mirror of Truth is to banish the Mist of Deceit with your own breath.

ELAINE: Let us hear the Oracle.

ORACLE OF THE GODDESS MEDUSA

Children, you are deceived! You see my terrifying head covering the Shield of Pallas Athena, my daughter, and do not realise I am the Balancing Power of Love. My Divine Head includes Mind and Heart. You need both. The Ordeal of the Labyrinth is to travel the path of the blue, eight-pointed Star, and the double axe of the moon. The star rays permit you to pass. Moon rays forbid. Each time you have to choose. Mine is the Alchemical Gold which flows in the Deities: Ichor - the Divine Blood in each one of you. I guide you in many guises. Hear my voice. I am Conscience and Wisdom. In Truth, you loved your drowned wife. You wish for her to forgive. When you have forgiven yourself, you have passed the test of the Labyrinth.

TRIAL OF THE LABYRINTH
TRANCE JOURNEY

ELAINE: It is necessary for you to enter trance. We will be with you.

PERCY: I find myself in a temple of Medusa. Two beautiful Gods are before me. The fair one says he is Lucifer-Hermes. The Dark one says he is Set-Eros.

LUCIFER-HERMES: Yes! I suppose you are astonished. I am a fallen Angel. As an intellectual, one needs to be periodically disillusioned. *(TALKING TO SET)* You create the illusion!

SET-EROS: So do you! In reality, neither of us does.

LUCIFER-HERMES: We tempt initiates with their own folly.

SET-EROS: I create sirens.

LUCIFER-HERMES: And I abstract causes.

PERCY: Hey! Don't talk over my head! I am the candidate. It is my soul you are fighting for.

LUCIFER-HERMES: Wrong! Only you create your own Divided Soul. We just help to give you discrimination.

ARIADNE: Excuse Me! Or do you just ignore women? I am Ariadne. I was divided between my husband Baccus and Theseus! And yet you ignore me!

SET-EROS: You have to learn to be interesting to get our attention.

ARIADNE: You have the arrogance of Byron and the conceit of Don Giovanni.

SET-EROS: Ariadne –You are like Melusine - half fairy, half dragon.

PERCY'S INITIATION
TRIAL OF SPIRITUAL CLIMBERS

LUCIFER-HERMES: You hope for a better world.

PERCY: I always have.

LUCIFER-HERMES: Look at these cloud pictures. What wonderful visions of Liberty, Equality, and Fraternity in action!

SET-EROS: You cover your eyes!

PERCY: Oh horror. What trick is this? The clouds are covered on blood. I see the slaughter of thousands!

SET-EROS: You are the fool. Sir Percival the pure of the Holy Grael.

PERCY: But where are my friends? Why don't they help? I cannot find them!

SET-EROS: Where were they in the reign of terror? Absent. Avoiding horror.

LUCIFER-HERMES: They were busy repairing the Temple of Lies.

PERCY: I see men, women and children slaving in factories. I see false villages, schools and universities. They are all dissolving.

LUCIFER-HERMES: While they are killing millions, they do not allow people free will to choose their own path.

PERCY: There is hope. Pallas Athena has unveiled the Medusa's Head. All deception vanishes. Hardly anyone passes the test.

PERCY: I see how I rebelled to spite my father - revenge for abuse, for flogging by my tutor. I could not cope with my wife, let alone two of them. The first punished me by suicide. The second described me as both Frankenstein and the monster. I created the monster myself.

LUCIFER-HERMES: Do you mind?

PERCY: Mind? Thank you. I am happy to fall with Lucifer if it is to fall from self-created delusions. But something strange is happening. Pallas Athena has put on the Mask of Medusa and now she is my second wife, laughing. She gives me her book Frankenstein, and I can laugh as well. She has forgiven me! I was both the professor and the monster. I created both!

PERCY ENTERS INTO ECSTASY SURROUNDED BY GOLDEN CLOUDS.

MEDUSA: Your initiation is not complete. You may not yet undertake the Trial of Passion. You are from a sphere of angelic reality and do not feel passion. You have come to share the Holy Grael of the New Aeon, the elixir of life.

PERCY RETURNS FROM TRANCE. THEY REALISE IT IS TRUE. THEY ALL DRINK FROM THE HOLY WELL AND SHARE IN PERCY'S ECSTASY. THEY GIVE THANKS TO THE DEITIES, AND BATHE IN THE SEA.

End of Rite.

THE FELLOWSHIP OF ISIS MANIFESTO

Growing numbers of people are rediscovering their love for the Goddess. At first, this love may seem to be no more than an inner feeling. But soon it develops; it becomes a longing to help the Goddess actively in the manifestation of Her divine plan. Thus, one hears such enquiries as, "How can I get initiated into the Mysteries of the Goddess? How can I experience a closer communion with her? Where are her nearest temples and devotees? How can I join the priesthood of the Goddess?", and many other such questions.

The Fellowship of Isis has been founded to answer these needs. Membership provides means of promoting a closer communion between the Goddess and each member, both singly and as part of a larger group. There are hundreds of Iseums and thousands of members all over the world, since the Fellowship was founded in 1976 by Lawrence, Pamela and Olivia Durdin-Robertson. Love, Beauty and Truth are expressed through a multi-religious, multi-cultural, multi-racial Fellowship. The good in all faiths is honoured. The Fellowship of Isis has no particular affiliations.

The Fellowship is organized on a democratic basis. All members have equal privileges within it, whether as a single member or part of an Iseum or Lyceum. This manifesto applies also to the daughter societies: the College of Isis, the Spiral of the Adepti, the Spiral of Alchemy, the Noble Order of Tara and the Druid Clan of Dana.

The Fellowship respects the freedom of conscience of each member. There are no vows required or commitments to secrecy. All Fellowship activities are optional and members are free to resign without question. Membership is free.

The Fellowship reverences all manifestations of Life. The God also is venerated. The Rites exclude any form of sacrifice, whether actual or symbolic. Nature is revered and conserved. The work of the Noble Order of Tara is for conservation of Nature.

The Fellowship accepts religious toleration, and is not exclusivist. Members are free to maintain other religious allegiances. Membership is open to all of every religion, tradition and race. Children, listed as "Children of Isis", are welcomed, subject to parental consent. The "Animal Family of Isis" accepts members' animal and bird friends through centres.

The Fellowship believes in the promotion of Love, Beauty and Abundance. No encouragement is given to asceticism. The Fellowship seeks to develop friendliness, psychic gifts, happiness, and compassion for all life. The Druid Clan of Dana develops Nature's psychic gifts.

The College of Isis has been revived after its suppression 1,500 years ago. Like Aset Shemsu, The F.O.I. itself, it has always been alive in the Inner Planes. It is from these Inner Planes that its return has been inspired. Magi degrees may be conferred through Lyceums of the College. Correspondence courses are offered. There are no vows nor secrecy.

Iseums are the very Hearths of the Goddess, or Goddess and God to Whom they are dedicated. These are listed, along with Lyceums. Tara Priories and Dana Groves are also listed regularly. All these centers are for FOI members only.

All members are equal, and are not subject to anyone. All work with the Goddess - or Goddess and God - of their own Faith. Every Being - human, animal, bird, tree - element - is an eternal offspring of the Divine Family of the Mother Goddess.

Made in the USA
San Bernardino, CA
09 December 2017